PENGUIN BOOKS
WIN YOUR INNER BATTLES

DARIUS FOROUX is the author of seven books, and founder of 'The Sounding Board'. A past student of business, he writes about productivity, habits, decision making, and wealth building. His ideas and work have been featured in the *Time*, NBC, *Fast Company, Inc.*, the *Observer*, and many other publications. Over 500,000 people read his blog every month, which he started in 2015 and uses as his main platform to connect with individuals across the globe who read his work or need guidance.

Learn more about him at www.dariusforoux.com

Also by Darius Foroux

Think Straight
Do It Today
What It Takes to Be Free
Highly Productive Remote Work
The Road to Better Habits
How to go from Procrastinate Hero to Procrastinate Zero

WIN YOUR INNER BATTLES

Darius Foroux

PENGUIN BOOKS
An imprint of Penguin Random House

PENGUIN BOOKS

Penguin Books is an imprint of the Penguin Random House group of companies whose addresses can be found at
global.penguinrandomhouse.com

Published by Penguin Random House India Pvt. Ltd
4th Floor, Capital Tower 1, MG Road,
Gurugram 122 002, Haryana, India

This edition published in Penguin Books by Penguin Random House India 2025

Copyright © Darius Foroux, 2016
Illustrations copyright © Darius Foroux
All rights reserved
10 9 8 7 6 5 4 3 2 1

The views and opinions expressed in this book are the author's own and the facts are as reported by him which have been verified to the extent possible, and the publishers are not in any way liable for the same.

Please note that no part of this book may be used or reproduced in any manner for the purpose of training artificial intelligence technologies or systems.

ISBN 9780143475071

Typeset By Digiultrabooks Pvt. Ltd.
Printed at Thomson Press India Ltd, New Delhi
For Sale in the Indian Subcontinent and South East Asia only

This book is sold subject to the condition that it shall not, by way of trade or otherwise, be lent, resold, hired out, or otherwise circulated without the publisher's prior consent in any form of binding or cover other than that in which it is published and without a similar condition including this condition being imposed on the subsequent purchaser.

www.penguin.co.in

CONTENTS

Preface   vii

Book One: Inner Warfare

Decide	3
Fight The Enemy Within	7
Know Your Enemy	9
What Makes You afraid?	12
Take Responsibility	15
Analyze and Improve	19
Do Not Worry About What You Cannot Control	21
What's The Worst That Can Happen?	24
Visualize	26
Commit To Improvement	27

Book Two: Control

Act	31
Build Confidence With Competence	32
Start Small	34
Stop Wasting Time	36
There Are No Wrong Decisions	38
Learn From Everything	40
Give And Do Not Expect Anything Back	41
Say No	42
Other People's Expectations	44
Eliminate Noise	46
Ways To Say No	47

| You Are Who You Spend Time With | 49 |
| Comparing Ourselves To Others | 51 |

Book Three: Purpose

In Search Of Meaning	55
What's Your Life About?	57
Finding Your Purpose	59
Practice Presence and Happiness	61
Enjoy The Moment	63
Stop Feeding Your Ego	65
Stop Thinking	66
Set Goals	68
5-step Method For Setting Goals	70
Type Of Goals	72
What To Do When You Fail To Achieve Your Goals	74
Your New-Found Purpose	76
Keep Repeating	78
Final Thoughts	81

Best of The Blog

Read This If You Worry A Lot	85
Are You Wasting Your Life?	90
25 Things About Life I Wish I Had Known 10 Years Ago	94
Slow Down: You're Not Falling Behind	98
How To Find Mentors	102
How To Build The Self-Confidence You Need To Win At Life	107
5 Way To Build A Thicker Skin So You Can Go Through Life Smiling	111
How To Read 100 Books A Year	116

Acknowledgements	121
Reading list	123
Newsletter	130

PREFACE

The book that's in your hands right now is my most important book. Not because it's the first book I wrote, which is something that means a lot as well. No, this is the book that generated the most emotional response with my readers.

Books often find you when you need them the most. And I hope this is the case with you and this book as well. I wrote *Win Your Inner Battles* after going through one of the most challenging times of my life. You'll learn more about that in this book so I won't go through the full story here in this new foreword. At that time, I felt stuck and powerless. I felt like my life wasn't going anywhere. And as a result, my mindset was so negative that I was perpetually stressed out. I experienced shortness of breath, couldn't get to sleep well, and was in a bad mood for days.

If you're in a situation that looks bleak right now, I want to share this: you're not alone. And it doesn't have to be permanent. You might not always have the ability or resources to change your surroundings, but you can always change your mindset. That's where personal success starts; from within.

When I started writing, I saw my life changing. And somehow, I felt like I should document how I overcame my inner battles with fear (I chose the new title because this book shows you how I won the battle inside my own head). For the first time in my life, I finally knew what I was doing. I had just quit my job at an IT research firm in London—a job that I took after feeling like I'd failed as an entrepreneur.

That feeling was completely unjust. In fact, I did well as an entrepreneur. After getting my master's degree in business administration by the end of 2010, I started a business with my dad. We grew the company fast. And after two years of doing that, I started a few businesses of my own. I got into consulting, building websites, and I even started a men's apparel brand (which failed miserably).

But because I didn't see the results I wanted to see, I thought I wasn't good at business. That was purely because of my inner battles. Somewhere along the line, I became my own worst enemy. You become too hard on yourself. You criticize yourself. And nothing is enough. You hate uncertainty. But here I was, just having quit my job, and I was committed to pick up right where I left my business.

I'd finally conquered the enemy within and I stopped chasing things I didn't want. I had clarity. And in this book, I will take you on the same journey I took to win my inner battles.

When I talk about the enemy within, I talk about fear and a lack of confidence. I believe those are the two biggest challenges that stand in the way of living life on your own terms. Since 2015, I've been truly living life on my own terms. I can tell you this: it's liberating. But it's not easy.

A lot has happened since I first published this book. By now, more than thirty million people have read my articles, nearly eighty thousand people are subscribed to my newsletter, and I've had more than four thousand students who took one of my courses. I also changed my mind about a lot of things. I believe that is a good sign. If you're the same person you were a year ago, something is wrong. That means you didn't grow.

But it wasn't all positive and great. I'm not the type that lies to other people. I also don't like lying to myself. I've done that for many years. And I'm done doing that.

I lost some friends that I believed were here to stay. They initially supported my ideas and concepts. But after a while, a distance grew between us. They preferred the status quo. I challenged it. That is not a good match. We grew apart.

I also experienced two health setbacks. On a business trip to Barcelona, I got a serious case of food poisoning after eating bad fish. That took out all the energy out of me, and it took me weeks to feel fit again.

And earlier that year, I also got a serious infection that needed to be treated with antibiotics. That stuff messes up your whole system. It took me almost a month to feel normal again.

For a person who wants to be productive, health is the most important factor. If your mind wants to work, your body must cooperate. A setback like that makes you appreciate your health. I noticed I became agitated. I stopped my usual daily habits. I worked too much and stressed about meaningless things (that's never a good sign).

I love to work, but the overall quality of my life is the most important factor there is. It's not money or status that I value. I value family, health, friends. But fortunately, I've created a great system in my life that quickly helps me realize when I'm losing track of the path to a purposeful life. And reading this book again, helped me to get back on track.

And that's when I *knew* it. This book is useful and deserved to be updated with what I've learned during that year and since. It helped me win my inner battles. And that's when I finally had the perfect title. A year later. Can you imagine that? You hardly get things right on the first try.

Life is not easy. And it's unpredictable. That will never change. The only thing you can change is how you manage your inner and external battles. But it all starts from within. Because if you don't win your inner battles, you will never truly live a good life.

A Whole New Book

This is not only an updated version of the first edition, it's a whole new book. I've completely rearranged the book to be clearer and more practical. But I've also kept a lot of things the same so you can see how much my style has changed. I initially tried too hard. I want you to see that. I used big words and tried to make the advice sound epic. That's not my style. I don't like to sugarcoat things and I always look at things for what they are.

But life is a process. After writing more than 150,000 words, I finally discovered my style. If you read this book closely, and are familiar with my blog posts, you can easily discover which parts are new, and which parts are old.

I'm forever grateful to everyone who read, shared, and commented on my articles. I am truly a student of you, the reader. Over the years, I've learned a lot from writing for you.

I hope you will find this book useful.

—Darius
May 25, 2021

BOOK ONE

INNER WARFARE

"If you know the enemy and know yourself, you need not fear the result of a hundred battles. If you know yourself but not the enemy, for every victory gained you will also suffer a defeat. If you know neither the enemy nor yourself, you will succumb in every battle."

—*Sun Tzu*

Feeling anxious when you experience turbulence while on a plane? That is normal. Not speaking up during a meeting? *Not* normal. If you are like most people, you are not aware of your deep fears. Every time you feel uncomfortable, you experience the same symptoms of real fear. Your heart beats fast, your palms are sweaty, maybe you experience shortness of breath. It is crucial to understand how our enemy operates. We all know how it feels to be afraid, or to experience stress and anxiety, but why do we feel this way? Once we know how our brains are wired and why we feel fear, we can start the battle.

DECIDE

"One can choose to go back toward safety or forward toward growth. Growth must be chosen again and again; fear must be overcome again and again."

— *Abraham Maslow*

Everyone on this planet dreams of becoming someone or achieving something. I've never met a person who didn't have dreams of becoming or achieving something when they grew up.

But most of us fear to follow our dreams because fear stops our journey towards success. Success has a different meaning for every person. The definition of success I use in this book is not related to money, however.

Sure, I aim for a rich life (full of love, experience, connection, and contribution), but it has nothing to do with money.

The ultimate reward of life is a tranquil mind, a mind that is free of fear, a mind that is confident, and takes on every challenge it faces. Success means we *experience* life instead of *enduring* it. Life does not have to be a struggle. But fear makes us suffer an inner war.

Fear once served as a mechanism that protected us. Nowadays, fear has turned into our enemy and it rips us of our freedom. When most people run into a roadblock, they quit.

What is it that *you* want? What are your goals? What are your dreams?

Many of us won't even begin the journey toward their goals because they are too afraid to start. Ralph Waldo Emerson put it best: "Fear defeats more people than any other thing in the world."

But what if I told you that it *is* possible to reach your goals? That you *can* make your dreams come true. You have to win your inner battles. Only then can you live life on your terms.

Fear is the enemy within that stops us from achieving our goals and dreams. We think that achieving greatness is for the select few. We think that people have been lucky. But that's not the case.

People who achieved their goals *decided* that they can.

Life is about making decisions. And giving into fear is also a choice. So let's not wait another minute. Let's start now. Let's defeat our fears.

Let's decide that we:

- Lead—not follow
- Create—not consume
- Stay positive—not negative
- Solve problems—not complain
- Bring joy—not melancholy
- Are powerful—not weak

Let's *decide* that we have the courage to do whatever we want. Say *no* to a life that is full of stress, anxiety, pain, hurt, sadness. Embrace a joyous life without fear.

You're selling yourselves short when you think it is impossible to live a fearless life.

We believe in the misconception that some people are born leaders, millionaires, artists. This is not true and believing this can do more harm than we think. People who are successful and live a fulfilling life all learned how to overcome their obstacles.

The night Michael Jordan was inducted into the Hall of Fame, he made a powerful statement that emphasized his fearlessness:

"Limits, like fears, are often just an illusion."

This illustrates Michael Jordan's refusal to be controlled by fear. He sees fear only as an illusion—*nothing more.*

We must defeat fear because it creates an inner war that hurts our confidence. This can be toxic—with too much self-doubt we will never pursue our dreams. We will become afraid to fail.

Instead of chasing our dreams, we get stressful when we face difficulty on the road. *We quit too early.* We feel anxiety when we think about what awaits us. At the same time, we think that we deserve more and get frustrated when our life lacks substance.

Happiness does not depend on your status or the amount of money you earn. Instead, happiness is achieved by progress and growth in life. However, when we are always in conflict with ourselves, we never grow.

Every single person who has achieved personal success or happiness, has learned how to overcome their obstacles. Instead of saying, *"I am just not that type of person,"* we must realize that everything in life is a skill.

And everything that is a skill, we can learn.

Even though we can and should defeat our inner enemy, one of the biggest truths in life is that we cannot have a completely fear-free existence. If we want to progress in our life, we must face our fears so that we can grow. It's a never-ending process.

Everyone has fear. What are you afraid of?

- Ending a relationship?
- Making decisions?
- Being alone?
- Intimacy?
- Changing your career?
- Failure?
- Losing face?
- What people think of you?

Every person on this planet has the potential to live a good life, and we are all blessed with talents and gifts. I'm not saying that just to encourage you.

But fear stands in the way of pursuing our talents and dreams. It is not the lack of resources that is holding us back, but the lack of confidence.

FIGHT THE ENEMY WITHIN

"Make sure your worst enemy doesn't live between your own two ears."

— *Laird Hamilton*

Conquering fear is important, especially now. We live in an interconnected world where the social pressure to conform to the norm is practically demanded from us. Many talented people take their talents with them to the grave because they are afraid to follow their dreams.

One of the main reasons is because of what we have learned from other people. From a young age, we are taught to be normal and follow the conventional circle of life: not to stand out, get an education, a safe job, get married and buy a house. We believe that it is so important to follow this path, that we are terrified to do something else.

For example, if you do not like your job, you live with constant stress. That impacts your mood, ambition, and above all, your health. Stress has severe consequences for our body.

Most of us spend our lives running from our fears. Conquering fear is liberating, and this new freedom will give you the energy to give back to the people you love.

The good news is that this is a simple skill. But similar to mastering every skill, it takes practice and the right set of tools. Everything starts with one realization: fear is a choice.

Research shows that 65% of our thoughts are negative and staying positive in today's world is almost a full-time job. You just have to turn on the TV, or open a news app on your smartphone, and you are confronted with fear-inducing messages instantly. We hear that the economy is bad, people are dying and about companies going bust. The general tone of the news is negative, which I understand.

Not everything that happens is pretty, but one thing is certain: the situation we find ourselves in is not because of external factors. We do not depend on our circumstances, so why do we let circumstances influence our lives? Fear of the bad economy, traffic accidents, or serial killers should not control our actions. After all, we do not control these things. However, we *do* have control over *our* actions and how *we* respond to life.

KNOW YOUR ENEMY

"Fear is the main source of superstition, and one of the main sources of cruelty. To conquer fear is the beginning of wisdom."

— *Bertrand Russell*

Maybe you fear public speaking, ending a relationship, standing up to your boss, losing your job, losing your money, asking someone out on a date, or going to the dentist. The list of common fears is endless. It doesn't matter what you fear specifically.

Understand this: it is natural to feel fear. Everyone has fear. But that's not important. It is more important to understand *why* we experience fear. This question is important because if you want to solve something, you need to be aware of it first.

The primary function of fear is to warn us of potential danger. Without fear, humanity would not survive. If a wild animal attacked you, fear would alert you, which triggers a fight or flee response. Fear's fundamental function is to protect you from harm.

Nowadays, we do not face so many looming threats as before modern civilization, but the fear mechanism is still a part of our system. Evolutionarily speaking, fear comes from our reptilian brain. And while we do not need fear in the same way anymore, evolution has not adapted our brain yet. It will probably take thousands of years before our fear mechanism adjusts to modern-day life. But the truth is that we no longer need fear to survive.

Let's face it: what dangers do we encounter these days? The threats we face are no comparison to the hunter-gatherer days from Man's earliest history.

In fact, life is easy, even when you compare it to several centuries ago. When we started the agricultural revolution, 10,000 years ago, people were killing each other over land every day. That continued for centuries. If it wasn't war that was killing us, it was an epidemic that would. We have only found cures for most diseases in recent history.

But things have improved now. Thousands of years of civilization have made life gradually easier. And fear is no longer protecting us but has turned into our worst enemy.

Your brain can't distinguish the difference between an actual physical threat, or a threat that's made up by yourself. The only thing that matters is to understand what fear feels like. Because that's the only way you can fight it, by knowing your enemy.

You're at war with yourself. To fight your inner enemy, you need self-knowledge.

Sun Tzu, the most well-known military strategist, put it best: "If you know the enemy and know yourself, you need not fear the result of a hundred battles. If you know yourself but not the enemy, for every victory gained you will also suffer a defeat. If you know neither the enemy nor yourself, you will succumb in every battle."

And to know yourself better, I've created a list of twenty questions that you can use to improve your self-awareness.

- What am I good at?
- What am I so-so at?
- What am I bad at?
- What makes me tired?
- What is the most important thing in my life?

- Who are the most important people in my life?
- How much sleep do I need?
- What stresses me out?
- What relaxes me?
- What's my definition of success?
- What type of worker am I?
- How do I want others to see me?
- What makes me sad?
- What makes me happy?
- What makes me angry?
- What type of person do I want to be?
- What type of friend do I want to be?
- What do I think about myself?
- What things do I value in life?
- What makes me afraid?

If you want to try this method, I would answer these questions with the first answer that pops up in your mind. As you can see, these are practical questions.

Please don't start a discussion about how you should interpret these questions. If you do that, we still be at it 80 years from now.

The truth is that everyone interprets these questions in a different way. And that's *exactly* the point.

For example: *What things do I value in life?* My answer is time, family, well-being. What was your answer? You see, there are no right or wrong answers.

No matter what you do, know yourself. You're both the warrior and the enemy.

WHAT MAKES YOU AFRAID?

"The purpose of our lives is to be happy."

— *the 14th Dalai Lama*

Fear, stress and anxiety have a significant impact on the quality of our lives. Living with fear, stress and anxiety causes the following:

- Living an unhappy life
- Long-term physical and mental impairment

It is not our purpose to live an unhappy life, full of fear, stress and anxiety. Fear is toxic. Fear is our greatest enemy. It rips us from freedom and paralyzes us. We use excuses to not face it, and we say things like: one day I will start that company, or, this time I will leave him/her.

Remember: fear is triggered when our safety is in danger. It is a tool to avoid physical harm and death from enemies. Now, ironically, fear itself is our biggest enemy. Historically, we live in safe times, and more often we are fleeing from ourselves than from actual danger. Fear is one of the main causes people are unhappy.

Not only will fear stop you from living a happy life in the present, it can also cause severe physical and mental problems in the future. Stress releases a hormone called cortisol. And cortisol harms your immune system.

As a result, you will become more susceptible to disease. Researchers have also found a relationship between cortisol and diabetes, osteoporosis, and heart disease. In addition, stress and fear can cause depression, bipolar disorder, panic disorder, and burn-out.

People have many different fears. What do you fear?

- Rejection
- Failure
- Change
- Accidents
- Losing your job
- Switching careers
- Aging
- Being alone
- Losing your money
- Not being able to pay the bills
- Getting ill
- Losing a loved one

After a closer look at the list, you can distinguish two different types of fear. The first type is the fear of something happening to us, such as an accident or illness. Alternatively, it could be something that requires us to act, like the fear of standing up to our boss. The second type of fear has nothing to do with external factors like a boss, or a drunk driver: this kind of fear originates from our inner state, such as the fear of being rejected. The fear of failure, vulnerability, and helplessness also fall into this category.

However, every type of fear we experience in our daily lives is based on one thought: *"I cannot handle it"*.

We are afraid we cannot handle the challenges of life such as rejection, failure, being alone or losing our money. If we *did* think we could handle it, why would we feel fear? Fear is more of an internal fight that we must deal with, instead of battling external factors.

This final thought paves the way of this book. If we believe we can handle all the challenges that life throws at us, we have nothing to fear.

Instead of, "I cannot handle it," say, "I *can* handle it."

This belief that you can handle everything that life throws at you requires you to look differently at fear. Fear is something that holds you back, instead of something that will protect you. With the set of tools presented in the next chapters, you can cope with the obstacles in life that cause you to feel fear, stress and anxiety.

TAKE RESPONSIBILITY

"Fear defeats more people than any other one thing in the world."

— *Ralph Waldo Emerson*

Horrible things will happen to us in the course of our lives. Everyone will, or has dealt with the loss of a loved one, losing their job, serious illness or disabilities. We will encounter things or events that cause stress or anxiety. It is a part of life. However, knowing that bad things will happen to us allows us to prepare. Moreover, the only way you can prepare is by accepting that it is not about what happens to you, it is about: *what you are going to do about it?* If something happens to us, we can sob about what or why it happened. However, that is a waste of energy.

Rather, focus on what you can do about it or what you have learned from that situation. Alternatively, when dealing with loss, focus on the beautiful things that the person has given us, and the experiences we shared and the things we have learned. Even though we have lost someone we love, we can keep their spirit alive by passing on the things we have learned from that person.

You are not the victim of your circumstances. Where you are in life is not because of the economy, your education or where you live. You are in your situation because of your choices and very likely because you give into fear. Do not throw in the towel on your dreams because of the bad circumstances you are in.

We often look at life for what it should be, instead of what it is. Everyone wants to have better luck in life. Being born in a wealthy family, with perfect looks. However, we have to live life with the hand that has been dealt to us. We have to take full responsibility for our current situation. You take responsibility by not blaming everyone else for your life. We all do this: we blame the economy, the place we live in, our family members, or our spouse. It is easy to blame someone else.

If you are unhappy in a relationship, there is no point in blaming your partner by saying or doing mean things. It is *you* who has decided to start a relationship, and it is *you* who is still in that relationship. Either enjoy it or end it, but whatever you do, never complain. It is the same for your job. If you do not like your job, do not blame your boss or coworkers. Take responsibility, it is you who decided to keep the job. There's no point complaining about your coworkers or your boss.

Marcus Aurelius, Roman Emperor from 161 to 180 and philosopher, said in his book *Meditations*: "Is your cucumber bitter? Throw it away. Are there briars in your path? Turn aside. That is enough." It can be as simple as that.

Next time you encounter a situation that does not make you happy, do one of the next three things.

1. Change the situation

Sometimes we can change a situation. If you have a conflict at work with a coworker, you could try to resolve that situation. By taking responsibility for what happened and proposing a solution, you can change your current (undesired) position.

Remember, we can only change so much. If you work in an environment where office politics and backstabbing is the norm, it is unlikely you can amend the culture unless you are a senior manager or the CEO. In circumstances where you do not have any influence to change it, you can do the following things.

2. Leave the situation

If you feel like you are in a situation that you do not like, leave it. For example, is your job making you miserable? Create a plan to leave the job. Do not storm into your manager's office and say, *"I quit, you bastard."* That only happens in movies. Start working on a plan and develop skills you might need to find another job. Believe in your abilities to find something else.

3. Continue, but stop complaining to ensure your happiness

To ensure your happiness, stop complaining. Complaining is poisonous for your mind. Taking responsibility means that you accept things for what they are. Once you accept something, you should not complain. However, if you do find yourself complaining, take this as a sign of not having accepted it yet. Because taking full responsibility means that you take even the negative things of your life as a learning experience.

Once you have taken action, accept the current situation. We often confuse taking responsibility with blaming ourselves. When you assume responsibility, you do not blame yourself. Everyone has a voice in his or her head that is extremely critical. It goes like this:

- "How could I be so stupid to fall for this guy?"
- "I'm such an idiot for taking shit from my boss."
- "I knew I couldn't trust her, I'm such a loser."

Do not worry, these thoughts are very common—but will become (or prove) unhealthy if you continue living in your current situation. If you start looking at life as a learning process, you will only gain from negative experiences in life. Thus, every mistake you make is part of your learning process.

Sometimes we even make the same mistake multiple times. That is still fine if you do not blame yourself. You do not deserve to be punished by yourself. Do not allow your negative thoughts to hold you back from living on. Most people blame themselves so much that they eventually quit doing stuff. For instance, they stop taking risks, and consequently, stop growing. If you do that, that means the end of your personal development.

Remember: it is not money that makes us happy, but progress. And without action, there is no progress. Living a stress-free life all starts with taking responsibility and requires you to not blame yourself.

ANALYZE AND IMPROVE

"For it is not death or pain that is to be feared, but the fear of pain or death."

—*Epictetus*

Stoicism is a school of philosophy that was founded by Zeno (c. 334 - 262 BC) in Athens. Stoicism is based on the idea that negative emotions are caused by misjudgments. In other words: if you experience a negative emotion such as fear, hurt, anxiety, it is because you did not make a correct judgment of the situation. And it is said that misjudgments cause unnecessary worry.

The Stoic philosophers believed that the goal of life is to achieve a state of happiness and tranquility. Because fear is one of the biggest obstacles to reach that state, the Stoics also wrote a great deal about fear. Some people think that what Stoic philosophers such as Seneca, Marcus Aurelius, and Epictetus wrote roughly 2000 years ago, is not entirely applicable to modern society. However, we are dealing with the same obstacles that they faced. Even though industrial revolution and the information age changed many things in the world, the way that humans behave and think is still the same. Seneca, who was the advisor to Emperor Nero, and lived ca. (c. 37 - 68 AD), said the following about a happy life:

"For what prevents us from saying that the happy life is to

have a mind that is free, lofty, fearless and steadfast—a mind that is placed beyond the reach of fear, beyond the reach of desire, that counts virtue the only good, baseness the only evil, and all else but a worthless mass of things, which come and go without increasing or diminishing the highest good, and neither subtract any part from the happy life nor add any part to it? A man thus grounded must, whether he wills or not, necessarily be attended by constant cheerfulness and a joy that is deep and issues from deep within, since he finds delight in his own resources, and desires no joys greater than his inner joys."

Seneca's quote is from roughly 2000 years ago. This highlights that every single problem or issue that we face already happened to someone else in history. Your problem is not unique.

Our misjudgments of situations often cause unnecessary fear or anxiety. Without having all the facts, we jump to conclusions and decide that something is stressful or is a problem. If we would only say to ourselves: *"this situation makes me feel anxious."* However, we make things even worse than they are by running and hiding from our fears, which causes even more anxiety. Our imagination goes wild, and before we know it, a small problem is turned into a mountain that we cannot climb.

DO NOT WORRY ABOUT WHAT YOU CANNOT CONTROL

There are many factors in life that we cannot control. Think about the weather, traffic, economy, terrorist attacks, accidents, death, etcetera. However, we do end up complaining and worrying about the things we simply cannot control. That is a waste of time and energy. Instead, focus on the things that you *do* control.

Imagine the following situation: You make a mistake at work that upsets a client. Maybe you send someone a wrong email. Maybe you forget to solve a problem. It doesn't matter what it is. Imagine that something goes seriously wrong at work.

What do you do when you find out? Do you stress out? Feel uncomfortable? Blame yourself? Blame others? Think it's the end of your career? When things go wrong, we become our own worst enemy because we focus on things we don't control.

It's one thing to read about these things. It's another thing to actually put it in practice. Because when shit hits the fan it's natural to panic. Instead of thinking, take a step back, and focus on what lies within your control.

Something else that causes us stress is worrying about what other people think about us. Thinking about these things is a waste of time and does not help you at all. About this, Marcus Aurelius wrote the following in his book *Meditations*:

> *"When you wake up in the morning, tell yourself: the people I deal with today will be meddling, ungrateful, arrogant, dishonest, jealous and surly. They are like this because they can't tell good from evil. But I have seen the beauty of good, and the ugliness of evil, and have recognized that the wrongdoer has a nature related to my own—not of the same blood and birth, but the same mind, and possessing a share of the divine. And so none of them can hurt me. No one can implicate me in ugliness. Nor can I feel angry at my relative, or hate him. We were born to work together like feet, hands and eyes, like the two rows of teeth, upper and lower. To obstruct each other is unnatural. To feel anger at someone, to turn your back on him: these are unnatural."*

People can only hurt you if you let them. Worrying about what other people say or think about you means that you let them. Live your life the way you feel is right and do not worry about what other people say. Do not let them hurt you. You cannot control what people think of you.

What do you control? Essentially, we only control our own actions and mindset.

We determine our:

- Desire
- Attitude
- Judgments
- Determination

That's about it. Anything else, we have no control over. So it makes no sense to worry about things that are not on that list.

That's a simple Stoic philosophy exercise. Something that has existed for centuries. And the best thing is that you can immediately apply this to your life. Next time you catch yourself worrying about a situation, focus on the things you control.

Do Not Worry About What You Cannot Control

What counts is that we do the right thing because that is all we can do. We don't control outcomes. Do you see?

- Made a mistake? Correct it.
- Something goes wrong? Find a solution.

Also, never be surprised when bad things happen. But rather expect them to happen. In that way, you will never be caught off guard. Instead, accept it, and then focus your energy on finding a solution. Always keep a positive mindset. If you want to live a purposeful and productive life, the most important thing is consistency.

Achievement is not about eureka moments, your big break, pulling off all-nighters, or drinking Red Bull all day. If you want to achieve things in your life, it's about aiming for daily progress. You want to exercise, read, work, learn, study, every single day.

Remember this: Inconsistency is the enemy of results.

And that's why I practice Stoic philosophy to improve my mental toughness. I don't want ups and downs because that hurts productivity. Instead, I want to progress 0.01% every day of the year. And that's a very realistic goal. Try it and maybe it will change your life too.

WHAT'S THE WORST THAT CAN HAPPEN?

Analyzing a situation that causes stress or anxiety begins with asking yourself the question: *what is the worst thing that can happen?*

Chris is one of the people I coach to defeat his fear. His biggest fear is to lose his job. He works in a psychiatric hospital as a care assistant. Chris recently found out that the hospital has fired some of the staff, as the result of decreasing government funding.

"I really like my job, and I do not want to lose it," said Chris in our first coaching session. Apart from the danger of losing his job, Chris and his wife just had their second baby. Many things are happening in his life.

I asked Chris, "what's the worst thing that can happen?" and he said, "I can lose my job."

"And?" I asked him.

"I have to go and find a new job."

"Is that a bad thing?" I asked Chris.

"Well, it is not the end of the world. I have found jobs in the past, and I am pretty good at my job. So I guess it is not a bad thing."

After getting all of the facts straight, the worst that could happen was that he could lose his job, get severance pay, and the hospital would probably help him find a new job. Moreover, he did not think that finding a job is the end of the world.

Thus I asked Chris, "why do you even worry?"

He laughed and said, "I do not know, I guess it is the paranoia that is caused by my co-workers. Not all of them are great employees you know, I think they are terrified of finding a new job. I would not even want some of them as my employee if I were a manager."

Unfortunately, this is often the case. Other people who have their fears and insecurities, project them willingly or unwillingly onto us. They project doubt into our minds.

Next time when you face a stressful situation, ask yourself the same question I asked Chris: *what is the worst thing that can happen?* We find out that the worst thing that can happen is not that bad after all. At a certain stage in life, we all had to find work. For people who want to end a relationship: we have all been single in the past. You will survive.

VISUALIZE

Once you have figured out what the worst thing is that can happen—envision that it will happen. Research shows that visualizing triggers a real response in your brain. In fact, when you visualize that something bad happens—your brain thinks it actually has happened. Your brain is not good at distinguishing whether something really happened or not. Consequently, your brain triggers a similar response when you imagine something. Visualization is an extremely powerful tool, used by the most successful people on earth.

Boxer Floyd Mayweather Jr is notorious for visualizing his fights in advance. Until now, the undefeated boxer has won 48 fights in his career and is widely considered to be the best fighter of all time in his weight class. After his fight with Manny Pacquiao in May 2015, deemed to be the bout of the century, Mayweather said, "I knew I had him from round one." It shows that Mayweather visualized himself winning way before the fight. When the actual fight came, he knew he would win. Again, after the fight, Mayweather was calm, since he knew he would win from the outset. He already experienced the whole event in his mind.

When we visualize something to happen, it almost feels like a déjà vu when it really happens. Visualizing something bad to happen is counterintuitive, but it will make us accept our fate. Once we accept it, we can improve it.

COMMIT TO IMPROVEMENT

If we want to have a successful career and a fulfilling social life, we need to commit to making that happen. Action follows commitment. Thus, without commitment we will never act. Commitment only takes us to say, "I can do this." This will give us more control over our life. When we gain control over our life, we start defeating fear, stress and anxiety. Fear cannot survive when it is not in control.

BOOK TWO

CONTROL

"I can control my destiny, but not my fate. Destiny means there are opportunities to turn right or left, but fate is a one-way street. I believe we all have the choice as to whether we fulfil our destiny, but our fate is sealed."

—*Paulo Coelho*

Without action there is no outcome. The best cure for fear is action. Always act with courage and dominate your enemy. Taking control means we take matters in our own hands—with full responsibility.

ACT

"When it is obvious that the goals cannot be reached, don't adjust the goals, adjust the action steps."

— *Confucius*

There are two guarantees in life. As everyone knows, life is not forever. However, the other guarantee is something that not many realize: if you do not take action there will be no outcome. The only certain outcome is that you do not achieve anything at all. Taking action is the most important step in conquering our fears. The good thing about taking action is that it is very simple: you can act or not.

Too often our friends, colleagues, coaches, managers tell us to take action. Or not to be afraid and go do something. At the same time, we read books and articles that give examples of all the great things that people have achieved. For instance, they say how much The Beatles practiced, or how much money Bill Gates made, or what a great inventor Thomas Edison was. But if it was so easy to take action, why isn't everybody doing it?

BUILD CONFIDENCE WITH COMPETENCE

What people do not tell you is that it takes confidence to take action. Some people have more guts than others but most of us need courage to take action. Creating confidence is the first step in taking action. You build confidence by learning new skills and competencies. You will notice your self-confidence rising once you master new skills.

I've researched self-confidence for years, and the most practical theory that I've found is something called 'confidence by competence.' In 1952, Bernice Milburn Moore published an article called 'Self-Confidence for Competence' in the journal of Educational Leadership. In the article, she discusses self-confidence for teachers, but I've found it useful in all settings of life.

If you look up the definition of self-confidence, you always get more or less the same description. Moore describes it as "a trust in self, a faith in one's ability to be able to meet situations as they may arise."

But more importantly, she says:

> *"Self-confidence without competence is of as little use as is competence without self-confidence."*

It means this: Going to business school is competence. But using your business competence to lead a company is self-confidence plus competence. They are only useful when combined.

That analogy goes both ways. Just confidence in yourself, without the competence, is also useless—talking the talk is not a sustainable strategy.

You need the talk and bravado, but you also need to develop the skills to back up your talk.

Building Your Self-Confidence

So you become more self-confident if you become better at what you do. That's the system, and it's backed by research.

How can you use this information? The following process is easy—but completing the steps takes hard work.

It goes like this:

1. Improve your competencies
2. Put them into practice
3. See results
4. Grow more confident
5. Repeat

That's the complete process.

START SMALL

It's easy to dream big and aim for big things in life because it happens in our imagination. But real life is difficult. However, starting small is easy. Once you write your first short story, blog post or build your first website or product, then things will be more manageable.

Of course, we should aim for big goals and strive for greatness. However, setting huge goals increases the chance of quitting. If you want to master a complete skill set, you cannot learn everything at once. Tim Ferriss mentions in his book *The Four Hour Chef*, that if you wish to become a master chef, you should just focus on cooking. When you have to spend your energy buying groceries, doing the dishes or anything else related to cooking, you are more likely to give up. Ferris recommends to get paper plates and plastic cutlery so you do not have to worry about cleaning up.

Apply this to what you want to achieve by making it easy to succeed at first. Do not do everything at the same time. Expecting world class skill from yourself is unrealistic. For instance, if you want to apply the things you learn in this book, it is easier to apply them on one aspect of your life first. If you focus on your personal life first, it is easier to correct the mistakes you make. It is impossible to learn something without mistakes. Also celebrate the small wins and give yourself a pat on the back when you managed to control your emotions next time when you feel stressful.

Breaking up your learning process in small steps is a good way of building confidence while developing your competencies.

STOP WASTING TIME

Imagine you are 90 years old and you are talking to your children, spouse, and grandchildren over Christmas dinner. One of your grandchildren asks, "many people say life is short. I thought I would ask you, granddad, because you are so old. Is it true? Is life really short?"

What would you say? If your answer is that life is really short, think again. The Roman philosopher Seneca argues that life is only short when you waste your time. We waste a lot of our time because we do not know how to use it. A life well lived is long enough.

How many times have you spent time with people you do not like? How many times have you spent your time on small talk and gossip? How many times did you go to a social engagement when you know you wanted to do something the next day? How many times did you waste a whole evening, watching TV shows? If this is the story of your life, your life will be short.

Seneca argues that we forget all these trivial things when we are on our deathbed. When we are on our deathbed, we probably would not think about how awesome season 2 of Mad Men was. We probably would think about the times we spent with our loved ones. The love, laughter, and connection. Those things are priceless in life. When you experience enough, life is long and fulfilling.

If you set a goal for yourself to become just a bit smarter, stronger and caring every day, you will have tremendous results in a year from now. You can do this by showing love and gratitude every single day. You can also spend time with the people you love and be 100% present. Give them your full attention and do not spend time on your smartphone. You can read for 30 minutes, every day. That is about 15-20 books a year, and that is when you read at normal speed. If you perform physical activity every day, like a 30-minute walk or go to the gym, you will be significantly healthier in a year. Not to mention how smart, healthy or caring you will be in 10 years. Progress is doing small things every day. Unfortunately, there are no shortcuts.

THERE ARE NO WRONG DECISIONS

When faced with tough situations, we often fear that we make the wrong decision. When we have a job we do not like, we think, "should I look for another job or wait for a promotion?" We do this all the time, with relationships, friendships, family, work, et cetera. As long as we look at a decision in a negative way, we will always fear making decisions. We focus on what would happen if we made a wrong choice. When facing a decision, this way of thinking assumes that there is a right and wrong choice. Unfortunately, we cannot predict the future and when you make a decision in the present moment, you have to make the decisions with the information you have.

When someone offers you a job, how do you know if it is the right decision to take it? Let's assume you take a new job because it pays better and offers better career progression. It is impossible to know with 100% certainty that you made the right decision beforehand. Maybe you will not like your new colleagues or manager. Maybe you find that the commute is tougher than you expected. However, you still made the right decision at that time. You simply could not predict the future.

When we adopt a mindset of "there are no wrong decisions," we do not fear making bad decisions. Every decision we make will lead us to opportunities to learn and grow. Regardless of the decisions we make, we simply cannot lose. If we lose our job, we are forced to find something else. We might meet the love of our lives at the job you were forced to find. What would happen if you were not fired? You probably would find her anyway, just not at that new job. This is win-win thinking. Every path we take offers valuable experiences. We just have to have faith that irrespective of which decision we make—our destination is the same. Everyone has a purpose in life, which path we take is up to us. Regardless of the path we take, we have to enjoy the experience and not fear that we made the wrong decision. That will cause us unnecessary stress and anxiety.

LEARN FROM EVERYTHING

We are too hard on ourselves and we think that mistakes are bad. The only thing worse than making a mistake is not learning from it. Everyone makes mistakes in life so there is no point in blaming yourself, or worse, blaming others. Instead, learn from everything you experience and make it your goal to learn. Learning contributes to our progress—the more we learn, the more competencies we develop. More skills imply more self-esteem, and less stress and anxiety. The keys to life are learning, progress and growth. Once we achieve that, we achieve success.

GIVE AND DO NOT EXPECT ANYTHING BACK

When we do someone a favor, people often do not show us gratitude. We feel offended or frustrated when this happens. We feel this way because we often convey kindness with the expectation of gratitude. However, people tend to be ungrateful. Dale Carnegie wrote the following in his book *How to Stop Worrying and Start Living*, about thoughtless people:

> *"It is natural for people to forget to be grateful; so, if we go around expecting gratitude, we are headed straight for many heartaches."*

In the same book, Carnegie even gives a shocking example of ungratefulness. He writes about a selfish lawyer, Samuel Leibowitz. Leibowitz had saved 78 people from going to the electric chair in his career. Not one of them took the time to thank him. 0 out of 78.

Next time we perform an act of kindness, give because of the joy that giving brings us. Marcus Aurelius put it best: "I do what is mine to do; the rest does not disturb me." We have to do what is right, and not worry about whether people would recognize it.

SAY NO

There was never any fear for me, no fear of failure. If I miss a shot, so what?

— Michael Jordan

We believe that we always have to say yes to opportunities. We fear that saying no leads us to miss out on money, fun, and other experiences. However, by always saying yes, we do not value our time. Blindly, we say yes to everything that comes our way. We often do not look at saying "no" as a skill or something that is essential to success and happiness.

If we are at work and our manager asks us to hand in a report before the end of the day, we say, "sure thing." It interrupts our work, and often forces us to push other things aside.

We say yes in our personal lives all the time. When friends ask us to go out while we have other things to do, we say yes. We do friends or acquaintances a favor, without thinking about it. We even say yes to bigger things that we do not want. For instance, we take jobs we do not like or start relationships with people we do not love.

Why do we do this? We are afraid to say no, to let people down and ultimately, to avoid confrontation. The stress of saying no often makes us say yes automatically. When we say yes reluctantly, we complain or blame ourselves, "why couldn't I just say no?" Moreover, with relationships, we are afraid that if we turn down an opportunity to settle down, another one maybe will not show up. We see this often with relationships at work. When you spend enough time with a person at work whom you feel (even slightly) physically attracted to, it is easy to start a relationship. When you start a relationship, you cannot 'kind of' want it. No, you should be in love.

OTHER PEOPLE'S EXPECTATIONS

Learning to say no can save us much time and stress. While we are afraid that we have to let people down, the opposite is true: people will start respecting you more when you start saying no. People perceive that as a strong character trait.

It is time to stop doing things in order to live up to other people's expectations. You do not have to do things you do not like. If you do not start saying no, and keep doing things you do not want to do—you begin to dislike the same person you are trying to please. Saying no not only benefits you, but also shows that you think about others. If you say yes to a night out with your spouse, while not feeling like it, you probably will not be in a great mood. It is not fair for your spouse if you are not mentally present. If you rather go out the next day because you are tired tonight, just say so. Your partner will respect you for that. If she does not, we have to explain why we say no. So encourage them to say no when they do not want to do something.

One of the reasons we find it difficult to say no is because we want to conform to other people's expectations. Sometimes we have to make decisions that will influence our life's outcome. In those cases, you cannot be afraid to say no. When parents expect their children to go to university, the children often give into the pressure. We are all unique and have things we want from life, so asking people to do something they do not like is not fair (no matter how badly you want it). If you do not wish to go to university because of a good reason, then do not enroll. We have to follow our passion and create our own path.

ELIMINATE NOISE

We should say no to everything that is noise. In his book *Essentialism*, Greg McKeown explains that the *'disciplined pursuit of less'* allows us to regain control over our choices. McKeown writes that many successful people in history were 'essentialists', people who can separate the essential from the non-essential in life. Saying no illustrates what you consider *essential*—everything you say no to automatically is noise.

About the importance of saying no, McKeown says, "yet as hard as it can be to say no to someone, failing to do so can cause us to miss out on something far more important."

When we want to live a stress-free life, we have to *choose* "no". Saying blindly yes to invitations from our colleagues, friends or family causes stress. We often regret saying yes for days. We worry about damaging our relationships. We worry that we burn bridges. We worry what people would think if we say no.

But the truth is that we live in an abundant world and by saying no you do not miss out on anything. The world is full of opportunity and beauty for you to enjoy. We think we are not good friends or colleagues when we say no. However, that is not the truth and you are not a bad person when you say no. Once we start saying no, we lose the fear of disappointing people and find out that it was not that hard after all.

We find that we replace the noise with tranquility and clarity. We enjoy the things we *do* say yes to more, and we become more present as a result.

WAYS TO SAY NO

It is not a crime to say no. Your friends and family will understand, they will still care about you, even when you cannot make certain social engagements. And if your friends do not get it, it is probably time to find new friends. When we truly care about someone we will still care about them if they miss an activity.

Besides, when it comes to a job, say no to everything that is not essential to your work. People will respect you for doing your job and not wasting time on meetings and coffee breaks.

1. The indirect "No"

Starting to say no can be awkward. Most people prefer to start with an indirect approach. In your personal life, you can say, "look, I want to join you for drinks, but I have to work on this project because it is important to me." When you start saying no more often, it is fine to make excuses so that you avoid saying yes. That is the primary goal when you start saying no. You do not want to do something, so find a way to say no without feeling uncomfortable.

2. The "Let me get back to you"

We are often caught off guard with invitations or requests from people. We feel the pressure to answer those requests immediately. Next time when you are caught off guard, often by phone or in person, tell them, "I just have to look at my calendar, let me get back to you about that." Alternatively, we can say that we have to discuss it with our spouse or family first before we can answer.

3. The conditional "Yes"

You do not always have to say no. When your boss asks you to collect information before the end of the day, you cannot say no to that. What we *can* do is to force our boss to prioritize. If you work in sales, for example, you can say, "I can give you the information, but that means that I cannot make the ten calls we agreed on today. Is that all right?" With this conditional yes, we force people to prioritize. It shows that you have other things on your plate.

4. The direct "No"

Once you are comfortable with saying no more often, you can take the ultimate step in mastering saying no. We give people excuses of why we cannot do something. We say that we cannot have lunch because of a "doctor's appointment". We feel socially awkward just to say, "I cannot make lunch this week." When you have mastered saying no, you stop giving excuses and start to say no firmly. Practice makes perfect.

YOU ARE WHO YOU SPEND TIME WITH

Jim Rohn, successful entrepreneur and author, said that, *"you are the average of the five people you spend the most time with."* By now, this is common knowledge.

It also has proved to be a common belief to many of the greatest minds. For instance, successful people like Tim Ferriss, Peter Thiel, Elon Musk, have all mentioned in interviews that you should be picky with whom you spend your time.

Human beings are social animals, and people have a massive impact on us. When you spend time with people who are negative, you will become negative as a result. Even if you are the biggest optimist in the universe: when you spend enough time with five pessimists, they will fill your mind with their pessimism.

Ever pitched an idea to a friend or family member and they said "Well, I do not know about that"?

They might say "How are you going to get the money to do that?" Or "How are you going to do this or that?" They will always find a reason *not* to do something.

When confronted with problems, pessimists will also focus on why the problem occurred instead of concentrating on the solution. Asking yourself *"why did this happen to me?"* will not help you. A pessimist will always find a reason why something went wrong.

Optimists, on the other hand, will encourage you. One great example of an optimist is Arnold Schwarzenegger. When Arnold auditioned for the role as "Conan", the casting directors asked him whether he could ride a horse. He answered with a firm *yes*. In fact, Arnold did not know how to ride a horse. Nevertheless, he got the role, and he learned how to ride a horse in time before they started shooting the film.

If you would go to an optimist with an idea or a problem, they would encourage you to chase that idea or to find a solution to your problem.

COMPARING OURSELVES TO OTHERS

On some level, we all want people to like us. Some even think it is their purpose to be liked by everyone. However, if you truly want to be free of fear, do not care about social approval or whether people like you or not. We are all unique, and from that point of view, comparing ourselves does not make sense. Everyone believes in the expression *"you cannot compare apples with oranges."* However, when it comes to ourselves we seem to throw the expression out of the window and compare ourselves to people on a daily basis.

For instance, we compare our car to the neighbor's car. We also compare our haircut, our clothes, our credit card, and our status. We constantly benchmark ourselves. We see these things other people have, and think we are not good enough because we do not have a platinum card, Porsche, $200 haircut, Christian Louboutin shoes, or anything else someone might have. All these things do not shape our characters and do not define us. They are merely food for our ego. Do not measure yourself by these things.

The way to keep yourself from this type of stress is to be driven by intrinsic motivation instead of extrinsic. Most people are motivated by external factors, which is not surprising. From an early age, we are influenced by our environments. Most people even build their whole life around external factors. This is also one of the reasons we fear to be different. When you are driven by intrinsic factors you have no benchmarks anymore, you have no one to compare yourself to. No salary, bonus or car from your competitor that you can measure yourself against.

This does not mean that we should never look at others. In fact, I encourage you to observe other people in order to learn, be inspired, or get motivated by them.

Think about what you value in life and pursue that. Making small or big decisions based on external factors is the recipe for disaster. Similarly, you should not automatically copy other people's behavior. The following is essential in this context: if you see yourself as a unique person, it is *impossible* to compare yourself to anyone else.

You are not better or worse than anyone on this planet. If successful people compared themselves, they would be miserable as well. We all have shortcomings or do not achieve greatness in every field in life.

Elon Musk is one of the most influential people on this planet, but he is not as powerful as the President of the United States. Lebron James is one of the best basketball players of all time but compared to Albert Einstein, he is not good in physics. Comparing yourself in this way is a bad idea. Do not focus on your shortcomings.

On the other hand, comparing can be a great thing sometimes. If you want to compare yourself, do it for the right things. Never be disappointed when you compare yourself to others. Instead, look at other people's achievements, work ethic or motivation to learn from them. However, if you feel you fall short, do not feel demoralized. Great people often look at other people to learn, especially when it comes to skills they want to develop.

However, be aware of comparing yourself on numbers. For instance, do not compare your Twitter followers to someone else's.

No one cares about those things but your ego.

BOOK THREE

PURPOSE

"To enjoy good health, to bring true happiness to one's family, to bring peace to all, one must first discipline and control one's own mind. If a man can control his mind he can find the way to Enlightenment, and all wisdom and virtue will naturally come to him."

—*Buddha*

What is purpose? What is meaning? Do we need it? By finding out our unique life's purpose, we can live a life that is full of substance. Having purpose strengthens our intrinsic motivation, which will help us to live a tranquil life. When we achieve freedom from fear, stress, anxiety, we can live a joyous life. We are too often cynical and pessimistic. By learning to practice joy, we will be happier in our life and relationships.

IN SEARCH OF MEANING

"Those who have a 'why' to live, can bear with almost any 'how.'"

— *Viktor E. Frankl*

It is difficult for most of us to talk about our purpose, since we often do not know what that is. Many thinkers have spent a great deal thinking, reading, meditating, and writing about how purpose is defined. One good book on this topic is from Viktor E. Frankl, a Nazi camp survivor. In his book, *Man's Search for Meaning*, Frankl writes about his time in a Nazi concentration camp. He explains why some prisoners of the Nazi regime struggled and others survived. Frankl used his experiences to create his psychological theory, Logotherapy. This treatment emphasizes how we can survive all circumstances in life as long as we have a personal meaning of life.

Frankl believes that the search for meaning is the greatest driver in our life. This gives the journey to finding your meaning importance as well. It is not the destination that matters, but it is the journey that is vital in our lives. Research from the Johns Hopkins University also confirmed this. Students were asked what they considered to be central in their lives. 78% mentioned that finding a purpose and meaning in life was most important to them.

Frankl warns us that if we give up on finding meaning or believe that there is no meaning to be found, we will live in an existential vacuum. This state leaves you feeling like your life has no meaning and is hollow. Unfortunately, more and more people live their lives in an existential vacuum these days. We get bored quickly in our modern world where we have so much spare time.

During the industrial revolution, people worked at least 12 hours a day. When the workers returned home in the evenings, they were tired, and all they wanted to do was rest.

Now, we have more time than ever, and we do not know what to do with all the spare time. We get comfortable in our lives and spend evenings watching TV shows and live for the weekends. People are always looking for ways to kill time.

Another side effect of boredom is that we start imitating other people. When you imitate others, you will find that your life is utterly devoid of substance. If the single reason you are doing something is because someone else is doing it, it is time to rethink your life. Time is your most valuable currency in life so spend it wisely. Imitating others is the way a poor man spends his time.

This is why people who are working on their passion say they did not take a holiday in years. These people often work seven days per week. However, for them, it is not perceived as work so they never get bored. It is their life's work and they are working to realize their personal meaning. You will see that if you find your meaning, all you want to do is spend time on things that will fulfill your purpose.

WHAT'S YOUR LIFE ABOUT?

Everyone on this planet has a purpose—our job is to find out what that is. Some people are destined to be great mothers or fathers. Some people are destined to be artists. Others are intended to help the less fortunate ones. We do not have to be world leaders to make an impact on people's lives. As a voluntary worker in a third-world country, you will help more people than any individual who sits at home, playing video games. However, you can give meaning to playing video games, as long as you are entertaining the world with your videos on YouTube, for example. It also proves to be a good source of making money.

The point is that everyone gives a different meaning to his or her life. Frankl says that one way to discover our personal meaning in life is by creating a "life's work".

You can give your life meaning by focusing on a goal. Many people think of names such as Steve Jobs, Thomas Edison, Albert Einstein, or Stephen Hawking when it comes to life's work. It is a good thing to look up to these people for inspiration. However, most people see their own life's work and say, "I am not Steve Jobs or anything."

With this way of thinking, you are comparing yourself to others. Your life's work can be raising your children in the best way possible. Your life's work can be to inspire children to read literature as a teacher. Your life's work can be writing children's books. No one expects you to cure cancer. However, if you feel like you can, do not think you cannot find a cure. Simply look at what you value most in life and make that your life's work.

When it comes to finding our purpose, some people argue that you first need a purpose to make the right decisions in life. I do not agree with this notion, since how we act towards *finding* our meaning is more important than *having* a meaning. It is impossible to find a general meaning of life for the purpose of your life depends on your decisions.

So why do you exist? If you do not know, that is great, start giving meaning to finding your purpose. If you do know why you are here, that is also great. Spend every waking minute on your life's work.

FINDING YOUR PURPOSE

Remember: purpose is a decision. No one is born with a purpose. It's something we decide.

Here's a question for you: **What *are* you?**

I'm not talking about your job title. What's your life about? Answer that, and you will have your purpose. But most of us don't have the answer to that simple question. We tend to overcomplicate things. But it's actually very simple.

Will Smith put it best when he was asked about this subject in an interview: "Just decide what it's going to be, who you're going to be, how you're going to do it."

Decide. Go out. Do it. And don't look back.

If you lack inspiration, and can't answer that question, you need more input. You can't expect to get output (purpose) without input.

You don't know your purpose because you're not aware of it. That's all. Don't make things more complicated than they are. And don't try to force it to come out of you.

Here are two ways to stimulate input:

1. **Expose yourself to different things.** Read about stuff you've never considered. Travel. Hang out with different people. The more you broaden your mind, the more information you get. New ideas are a blend of existing different ideas that you're exposed to.

2. **Manage stress and anxiety.** Chronic stress and anxiety prevent your mind from thinking in a clear, focused, and a relaxed way. Those are key ingredients of getting new insights. So before you think about finding your passion, deal with stress and anxiety first if you're having a lot of it.

Instead of consciously thinking about your purpose, you can try an indirect approach. Just realize that your purpose is inside of you, it's just afraid to expose itself.

You must trust that someday it will seemingly appear out of nowhere. When that day comes, do a happy dance, celebrate, whatever, but the next day, wake up and start working on your purpose.

PRACTICE PRESENCE AND HAPPINESS

"If you want happiness for an hour—take a nap.'
If you want happiness for a day—go fishing.
If you want happiness for a year—inherit a fortune.
If you want happiness for a lifetime—help someone else."

— *Chinese Proverb*

Happiness is a skill. Mastering that skill starts with managing your thoughts. People believe that you cannot influence your thoughts. Do you think about the past all the time? You're not the only one.

In fact, most people's thoughts are similar to cinemas that play old movies over and over again. What will you accomplish by replaying a nasty breakup in your mind? Or, that one time when your manager yelled at you? That is in the past, and you cannot do anything about it.

Similar to influencing negative emotions such as anger, regret, frustration, you can control joy as well. We think that our emotions determine our mood. That is only true to a certain extent. It is also true that we influence our emotions by our thoughts. So this goes hand in hand, and it means that you can control joy by thinking and acting happy. Some people are always cynical and believe that being happy is for children or naïve people. They are utterly sad and often argue that they are being realistic instead of pessimistic. Remember: the goal of life is to live a happy life. Being cheerful makes life 10x better than it is.

Next time, when a negative person or a bad situation confronts you, do not worry about it for too long. Instead, always focus on the positive things. Even if you are in a situation you do not enjoy, try to think of something you do like about that situation. For example, when you lose a loved one, think of all the beautiful memories you have of that person. When you are stuck in traffic, which causes you to miss an important meeting, enjoy some of your favorite music or listen to an audiobook in your car. There are many things in life you simply cannot influence. So, instead of worrying about them, see the good in bad situations.

Being negative is easy and everyone can be cynical. However, staying positive is more difficult and requires persistence. When we adopt a positive mindset for our life, we start creating our reality. Using positive thoughts makes us strong, while negative thoughts make us weak. Dealing with obstacles becomes easier when you believe that there is *always* a solution, regardless of the severity of your situation. If you think you cannot find a solution, chances are you will be unsuccessful.

However, when we commit to a positive mindset, we empower ourselves, which eliminates fear, stress and anxiety from our lives.

ENJOY THE MOMENT

By focusing on the present, you can ignore the past or future. Many want to find inner peace and turn off the voice in their head. By being fully present you can achieve a state of mind that is free of worry. Living in the present will also free you from any fear. Because there is no fear when you truly live in the moment (unless a tiger is charging at you at this very instance). Our most common fears concern things or events that might happen in the future. We tend to live our lives in the past or the future. If you are not worrying about what might happen, you are either reminiscing or regretting the past. When you do this, you neglect the present.

When you are physical with your spouse, but your thoughts are with work, you are not present. Your partner deserves your full attention. The present is important because life does not occur in the past or future. Things happen before our eyes and if we do not pay attention, we miss a moment that will be forever gone.

Events occur in a flow of present moments. Even when you replay a feeling from the past, that feeling was once experienced in the present—therefore, when you say that something happened in the past, that is not true. When something occurs, it always happens in the present. Your memories also occurred in a moment that once was the 'present' for you.

Worrying about the future or dwelling on the past will yield nothing, whereas living in the present moment will. If you manage to live in the present moment, you will experience neither stress nor anxiety. There is no reason to fear something that has not happened or regret something from the past. You have no control over those things. Similarly, worrying about looming deadlines can create excessive anxiety. Instead, focus on solving one part of the problem at a time. By deconstructing your challenge and dealing with them step by step, you take care of your problems in the present moment.

You might wonder, "how can you enjoy the moment when something bad occurs to you?" If something happens that causes stress and pain—that is very real and it happens in the present moment.

Eckhart Tolle writes, in his book *The Power of Now*, that the stress you experience when something bad happens is self-created inner resistance to external factors that we cannot change. As a result, we experience pain because we are unsatisfied and powerless about a situation. When we experience a situation that frustrates us, we feel anger, and that anger will constrain our ability to think rationally.

This frustration will in turn lead to more stress—we say things like "How could I let myself go like that?" This thinking pattern is a negative cycle that will lead to more stress and anxiety. Mental suffering is always self-created and comes from inside yourself. That means you can also decide to stop it. Life is not meant to be suffered. It's meant to be lived, enjoyed, loved, and truly experienced.

STOP FEEDING YOUR EGO

The main thing that stands in the way of practicing happiness is our ego. Our ego controls our thoughts and behaviors, without us realizing it. Most people are not aware of their ego, which makes it difficult to control their happiness.

Ego is also a problem in relationships. What is more important in your relationship: winning arguments or true love and connection? With many relationships, it looks like winning arguments is more important than love, connection, affection, support, and having a good time with each other. Next time when you are getting into an argument, stop and ask yourself whether *you* or *your ego* is having the argument.

STOP THINKING

Once you realize that your mind and ego are causing you stress and anxiety, you need to separate yourself from both your mind and ego. The way to detach yourself from your thoughts and ego is by becoming fully conscious of your mind. Your mind is more powerful than you think. If we do not understand it, our mind will control us. You can detach yourself from your ego by observing your mind and thoughts.

The following exercise helps you to achieve this:

1. Remove yourself from your thoughts

After you are finished reading for today, start with observing your thoughts from a third person perspective. Picture yourself looking at what your mind is thinking. Just observe when your mind wanders off to the past or future.

2. Accept your thoughts

Do not judge your thoughts, this exercise is all about observing. You will notice that you are almost constantly thinking about something, and nearly 90% of those thoughts are about the past and future. This voice in your head is a massive cause for your self-inflicted stress and anxiety. Now, accept that your voice exists and know that you do not have to follow it.

3. Ignore your thoughts

Instead of following your thoughts—stop yourself when you notice that you are being unreasonable. Otherwise, you end up like a dog that is chasing cars. For example, when you agreed to have a call with your friend at 7pm—and she does not call you, do not judge her. *Stop following your thoughts.* She might be in the middle of something—you do not know the reason she has not called you yet, so do not worry about it.

Eventually, you will find yourself in control of your mind and this will make you stop thinking about the things you cannot change, or trigger your worry.

SET GOALS

"The greater danger for most of us isn't that our aim is too high and we miss it, but that it is too low and we reach it."

— *Michelangelo*

I have a love/hate relationship with goals. I hate goals because they cause tunnel vision. I love goals because they give you a sense of direction.

The most important thing about setting goals is that it's not about *achieving* the goal. It's about the process that leads you to the goal. I can assure you that you won't get lasting happiness when you achieve your goals. Have you ever set out a goal, achieved it, and thought, "now what?" That is what I'm talking about. It's not about achieving the goal. It's about how the goal changes your daily life. Striving for goals forces you to form new habits. And that's priceless.

If you want to truly defeat your inner enemy, you need a purpose. Your purpose will help you to be less anxious about the future because you have a conviction. However, without a clear set of goals, you will fail to fulfill your purpose. A thought *must be executed* and by setting goals, you can start acting on your purpose. Execution is the only thing that brings a change to your life.

And goals are a way of actively seeking out our ambitions. Before starting to chase your dreams, start by defining your goals

Set Goals

as precisely as you can. If you do not have goals, make them up. Everything is better than having no goal at all. Even if you do not know what you want to do with your life, you have a goal: to find out what you wish to do with your life. Some people say, "I am not an ambitious person." No one is born with ambition or predefined goals. Ambition is a conscious decision to pursue growth in life, through experience or achievement. Even if you have a purpose, without goals, your life is still aimless because your destiny seems so far away or intangible.

Goals are made up, and if other people can make up goals, then you can do it too. When set correctly, goals will guide you to your destination. For example, if you want to change your career, set clear goals for yourself. Ask yourself questions like, "what does my ideal job look like?" and, "when do I want to quit my current job?" By asking these questions you find out what your path looks like. From the answers to those questions you can set goals. For instance, "I want a job with enough freedom to express my creativity." And, "I will give myself six months to quit my job and find my ideal job."

Another reason we set goals is because we cannot just sit around and hope that something good will happen to us. 'Hope' is not a strategy. Hope is for people who have high expectations but are not willing to do anything to make their dreams happen. After all, it is easy to do nothing. Reaching your dreams requires determination— and achieving your goals is tough. You will be rejected, you will fail.

However, you cannot give up, for every setback teaches you something. And when you do complete your goals, the victory will be greater.

5-STEP METHOD FOR SETTING GOALS

1. Be precise

"I want to be rich," is not a specific goal. You should decide how much money you exactly want to make. For instance, if you wish to lose weight, you should decide exactly how much you want to weigh.

2. Think big

Do not play it safe. A life that is played safe is not a life worth living. Remove all limits you have in your mind and think about what you truly want to achieve. We are our greatest enemy when it comes to goal setting. The voice in our head says, "that is way too outrageous," too quickly. Turn that voice off and always aim high with everything that you do.

3. Set a deadline

It is important to determine when *exactly* you want to achieve your goal. A goal is pointless if you will achieve it "someday". If you want to move to New York City one day, mark a day in your calendar. For example, June 1, 2018: move to NYC. Otherwise, your goal will float somewhere in the undetermined future. Chances are you will never accomplish a goal that has no deadline. In addition, looking at the date on your calendar motivates you to work toward your goal.

4. Decide what you will sacrifice

Achieving goals without sacrifice is a myth. You cannot lose weight and eat whatever you want, whenever you want. You have to make concessions. Think about things that you have to sacrifice. You do not have to give up everything to accomplish your goals. If you wish to lose weight, you can eat whatever you want on your 'cheat day'. Commit to what you want to sacrifice and mentally prepare for it. For instance, if you aspire to be a musician, chances are you have to travel to perform. Thus, mentally prepare for not seeing your family and friends all the time.

5. Write down your goal and action plan

Write down your goal in clear and short sentences. Your action plan does not have to be detailed when you are setting your goal. It needs to contain steps that you will take to achieve your goals. It can be as simple as, "read a book per week."

TYPE OF GOALS

Apply the specified 5-step method for setting financial, personal, learning, and health goals.

Financial Goals

Calculate the exact amount of money you need for the lifestyle you desire. Do you want to go on a holiday four times a year? Calculate how much that will cost as accurately as possible. Consider everything that you want to do or buy. Finally, take your monthly liabilities into consideration. Adding these figures up, gives you a total amount of money you need to live the lifestyle you wish.

Personal Goals

These are the things that you want to do before you die. Also, you can set goals for the person you want to be. We decide what kind of person we want to be— the person we are is completely in our control. Think of Marcus Aurelius, Emperor of the Roman Empire—his goal was to always do the right thing and treat people fairly.

Learning Goals

Knowledge is the starting point of every challenge you take on. Many confuse knowledge with school. While school often teaches us things we are not interested in, we should take personal responsibility for the things we learn and are curious about. This has nothing to do with school and is a commitment to life-long learning.

Knowledge is one of the most important aspects of human evolution, if not, the most important. Knowledge is what helps us survive and adapt to any threat we face. We can learn from the mistakes that others made through books. People learn in different ways: documentaries, books, school, audiobooks, podcasts, mentorships, or interviews. Find out how you learn and set goals for what you want to learn and how you are going to do it.

Health Goals

This is about the body you want and the physical condition you want to be in. With a healthy body and mind, you can take on every challenge that you face. Dr. John Ratey shows in his book *Spark*, how regular exercise can lower the chances of atherosclerosis, diabetes and depression. Additionally, regular exercise improves your immune system so you are less susceptible to diseases. We have been given a body, and it is our job to develop and maintain it.

WHAT TO DO WHEN YOU FAIL TO ACHIEVE YOUR GOALS

Goals are perfect for setting direction. But, they will not do the work for you. To get work done on a daily basis, you need to rely on a system.

The benefit of a system is that it cannot fail. Do you know that feeling of setting goals and not achieving them? It is not a good feeling. We feel defeated and worthless.

That's why I'm an advocate of backing up your goals with a system. A system is nothing more than a recurring process. Create a daily recurring process that will bring you to your goals. For example:

- Want to get rich? Add value to other people's lives.
- Want to get recognition? Do great work.
- Want to win a race? Train hard.
- Want to be happy? Don't take life too seriously.

In the end, only *you* can create a system that supports your personal goals.

Now that you have the tools, you can create your own system. Having a system, and focusing on the daily progress, will prevent you from forming tunnel vision. Because sometimes, it's easy to blindly focus on a goal that you've once set out to achieve. For example, a lot of people want to make a million dollars a year. It's something that's popularized by modern culture. But why do you want a million dollars? If you keep focusing on that goal, you might get yourself into a situation that you don't like. You might say yes to work that does not align with your values. And you might get a lot of stress because of that. The question you want to ask yourself is: why am I striving for a goal? And you want you ask yourself that regularly. Otherwise, you risk achieving goals that will not improve the quality of your life.

Even when you do achieve your goals, do not expect fear to go away. For instance, many professional actors are still afraid every time they take on a new role. Just look at the celebrities who throw up backstage, or sometimes even on stage. A random Google search shows you that some of the biggest names in show business experience some sort of stage fright. Rihanna, Justin Bieber, Lady Gaga are all reported to vomit backstage. Or even during a performance. Adele, Grammy-winning artist, told Vogue magazine, "I puke quite a lot before going on stage. Though never actually on stage. I shit myself before everything. The bigger the freak-out, the more I enjoy the show!"

Win or lose, success or failure, fear will always stay. You better learn how to fight it.

YOUR NEW-FOUND PURPOSE

"We must build dykes of courage to hold back the flood of fear."

— *Martin Luther King Jr*

When it comes to our inner battles, it is not the goal to run away because that will lead to more hurt. Life is difficult. That will never change. Once you deal with one obstacle, another (often bigger) challenge is waiting for you. But that's exactly what life is about. See? Life is not about hiding, running, or shying away from conflict. It's about meeting your adversity head on.

Those things sound great on paper, right? You read it and think you're ready to face life. But unfortunately, that's not how it works. No matter how many personal development books you read, you still have to toughen up and become a warrior.

Through serious introspection, and by engaging with thousands of people over the years, I have found one simple thing. Life is a lot easier to bear when you have conviction.

Once you know where you're going (even when you've made up your direction), you keep moving forward. And that is the only thing that counts. Do not worry about making the perfect decisions, just *decide*. Because once you get going, you can always go in a different direction.

Remember this: life is not something that you can figure out. There is no right or wrong. There is only YOUR life. Own it.

KEEP REPEATING

"The separation of talent and skill is one of the greatest misunderstood concepts for people who are trying to excel, who have dreams, who want to do things. Talent you have naturally. Skill is only developed by hours and hours and hours of beating on your craft."

— *Will Smith*

"I've read this book. Now I've conquered my inner battles once and for all." If you think that, you couldn't be more wrong.

Your brain is a muscle that requires permanent training. If you're a runner, you don't run one 10K race and quit forever, do you? If you want to master your inner battles and become mentally tough, you have to keep training your brain. And the only way to train your brain is to repeat the things you learned. Just like strength training, intellectual strength is about making reps. No one goes to the gym, bench presses one time, and goes back home.

David Schwartz, author of *The Magic of Thinking Big*, describes our mind as a bank where we deposit thoughts that we will access later. He argues that we become what we think. If we deposit positive thoughts in our mind, we will access them when we face difficulty along the road. Instead of giving up we will automatically think positive. We reap what we sow.

By knowing that we can control any kind of emotion and information we store in our mind, we determine who we become by controlling our thoughts. That is why it is important to be optimistic. We need it when times are tough.

Not matter what your circumstances are, you determine your mindset. This notion sounds rather simplistic on paper but is quite difficult to sustain over time. Remember: it is easier to be pessimistic. The difficulty of maintaining a positive mindset is also because of internal and external factors. Next to your own negative thinking, outside factors such as the media, or the people you spend time with, also influence your mindset. Most people are inherently pessimistic, sometimes even without realizing it. Most people think small and only gossip about other people. If you do not watch out, you will become like everybody else. The fear of giving in to normality is something you actually *should* be afraid of.

As an experiment, keep a journal for one day and write down all the messages you receive from all media and people you encounter. Include all forms of communication: in person, radio, Facebook, Twitter, WhatsApp, television, et cetera. Write down everything you see and hear. The easiest way to do this is with a note-taking app on your smartphone.

You will find that most of the messages you receive, strengthen your thoughts related to fear. Maybe you talk to your mother who says, "be careful driving home tonight," or maybe you read a news article titled "Two People Killed During a Robbery". You might hear on the radio that, "people's pensions are worthless these days. People lost billions of dollars during the previous economic crisis. It will happen again!" When you are at work you might hear that, "John was laid off, and no one knows why."

Fear. Fear. Fear. All these messages induce fear. Negative messages are more toxic than you might think. In a study by MIT, researchers found that for every time you hear 'you cannot do it' you need to hear 17 positive affirmations to overwrite or cancel out the original negative message.

Fear and negativity surround us, and you need to arm yourself by training your mind.

The only way to do it is to be aware of your inner battle. You can never slip up. You always have to be prepared for battle.

FINAL THOUGHTS

Before you are a leader, success is all about growing yourself. When you become a leader, success is all about growing others.

— Jack Welch

The world needs more fearless people—*more leaders*. Take a look at your surroundings. Inspect your relationships with friends, family, colleagues. Look at your workplace. *How many leaders do you see?*

Holding a senior position does not make one a leader. Someone with a title, only has power over non-factors—they do not inspire. They might tell us what to do, but they do not challenge our mind. Often, people follow them because they *have* to—not because they *want* to follow.

The world is in need of people who inspire change. People who take initiative. After all, we have enough *victims*. So decide to be a leader by:

- Inspiring people
- Making others feel good about themselves
- Setting a good example
- Amplifying positivity
- Solving conflicts

- Standing strong amidst crises
- Radiating love
- Becoming fully present
- Committing to life-long learning
- Taking care of our body and mind

As a leader, we *give*. Some people might wonder, *"what's in it for me?"* Zig Ziglar said it best: "You can have everything in life you want, if you will just help other people get what they want."

We all know it: the most beautiful things in life are free. But there is one condition—to receive, you need to give.

Challenge yourself to experience as much as you can. Commit to life-long learning and growth. Give, but also be open to what people want to give you. That's the heart of a warrior with a tranquil mind—free of any fear.

BEST OF THE BLOG

The most read articles from <u>dariusforoux.com/blog</u>.

READ THIS IF YOU WORRY A LOT

The day that I decided to quit my last job and the day that I handed in my notice were almost 90 days apart. In those three months, I worried—a lot. I decided to pursue my desire to become a full-time writer. But shit was getting scary.

Things like "what if I can't pay my bills?" and "what if I fail?" went through my head. I freaked out, but as it turned out, the solution to my excessive worries was easier than I expected.

Many of us worry about all kinds of things: Work, relationships, money, health. Some concerns are real, but many are unnecessary.

No matter what kind of worry you have, the response in your body is always the same: It increases your cortisol levels.

And an increased cortisol level is something you definitely *do not* want. Cortisol compromises your immune system. As a result, you will become more susceptible to disease.

Researchers have also found a relationship between cortisol and diabetes, osteoporosis, and heart disease. Also, stress and fear can cause depression, bipolar disorder, panic disorder, and burn-out.

Let's face it: If you don't stop worrying, you will die. That's not me talking. That's your body talking.

In the past year and a half, I've studied worry, stress, fear and anxiety almost every day. I even wrote a book about how you can live a stress-free life (*the one you're reading now*). My findings?

Don't try to relieve stress and worry, but eradicate it. Address it — head on.

> *"Fear defeats more people than any other one thing in the world."*
>
> —*Ralph Waldo Emerson*

Relief Doesn't Work

This is what most people do when they experience stress and worry:

- Take it out on our partner or family
- Drink alcohol, take drugs, or both
- Binge-watch Netflix
- Play video games
- Go on a holiday
- Party all night
- Have sex

Be honest, how long do these things make you forget about your worries? 10 minutes, half an hour, a full day? It doesn't last. As soon as you get back to the reality of your life—worry and stress smack you in the face.

Distracting yourself from your life doesn't work—and yet, many of us keep doing it. I've read many books and scientific papers on this behavior. Some say it's because we have too much free time, some say it's because of culture, some say it's because how we are wired.

To be frank, it's not important to understand the *why*. We just have to look at the facts: People worry too much, and that can destroy your life. It's more important to focus your attention on addressing worry.

"Never let the future disturb you. You will meet it, if you have to, with the same weapons of reason which today arm you against the present."

— *Marcus Aurelius*

Turn Worry into Constructive Process

Worry is often about the future. It goes something like this: What if…

- "She doesn't like me anymore?"
- "I lose my job?"
- "I can't pay my bills?"
- "I fail this exam?"
- "I don't get this promotion?"
- "My business doesn't take off."

And then we make up consequences. It goes something like this: I have to…

- "Be single."
- "Find a new job."
- "Borrow money from my parents."
- "Quit school because I failed."
- "Stay at this job another year."
- "Be ashamed because everyone thinks I'm a failure."

Then we think: "I can't handle that." And finally, we think: "The world is going to end."

If your thought process is the way described above, worry controls you.

The good news is there is a simple solution: Self-monitoring, which turns worry into a constructive process. In a 2002 study, done by Szabo & Lovibond, students were asked to record their worries.

The results of that study demonstrated that you can turn worrying into a constructive process by focusing on finding a solution to your concerns.

> *"You have to learn the rules of the game. And then you have to play better than anyone else."*
>
> —*Albert Einstein*

How I Use Self-monitoring To Address Worry

I'm a pragmatic person. I do think that things like meditation and mindfulness help with worry—but not for me. It's too intangible. Instead, I prefer to take a practical approach like self-monitoring. Here's how I do it.

1. **Use a note-taking app and create a new note.** I call my note "Things that I worry about."
2. **List everything you worry about—and keep adding things to the list.** Everything that you worry about goes on this list, no matter how small.
3. **Think of a solution to all your perceived problems.** For example, if your financial situation makes you anxious, you need to create a plan to earn more or spend less.
4. **Then, start executing.** Do one thing every day that brings you closer to solving your perceived problem.
5. **Finally, don't worry about things you have zero control over**—those things you have to accept.

If you want to know more about how you can do this; read *Meditations* by Marcus Aurelius.

This process focuses on action. It forces you to learn the skills you need to overcome your perceived problems. Because problems don't disappear out of themselves.

Nowadays, I don't worry anymore because I trust my ability to handle everything that life throws at me.

Because knowledge, skills and character are the only things that no one can take from you—every minute you spend on learning something is well spent.

No matter what happens, trust in your ability to address it. So start now.

ARE YOU WASTING YOUR LIFE?

"You're not your job. You're not how much money you have in the bank. You're not the car you drive. You're not the contents of your wallet. You're not your fucking khakis." That's one of my favorite lines from one of my favorite books: *Fight Club* by Chuck Palahniuk.

I've read *Fight Club* probably five or six times. But when I reread it again recently, that line really hit me. Are you wasting your life if you try to chase all those things?

In the midst of our pursuit of whatever we're after, it's easy to get so distracted that we lose sight of what matters—and before we know it, we waste our time chasing the wrong things.

It's fine to set goals and pursue things in life. However, you don't *need* whatever you're pursuing to live a meaningful life. Here's why.

You Are Not Your Bucket List

Don't trick yourself into believing you *have* to do crazy shit just make it count. It's all useless if you keep going from one thing to the other so that you can cross things off your list, and can talk about it at parties.

We buy things, we party, we jump off cliffs, we go on holidays, we move to different cities, we switch jobs—but nothing changes inwardly after we've done those things.

I'm not saying you shouldn't have a bucket list. But we should realize that we can live a meaningful life without one. Don't put pressure on yourself *just to do things*. Who cares? Your life is not a Nike slogan.

You can live with very little and be happy. With that realization, you can go and do the things that you truly want and not just because some article that says: 10 Things You Should Do Before You Die.

> *"Very little is needed to make a happy life; it is all within yourself, in your way of thinking."*
>
> *– Marcus Aurelius*

You Are Not Your Social Status

College degree, job title, number of friends and followers, are all means to measure ourselves. Somehow, we need to determine where we stand in society.

Are you a winner or are you a loser? That's what we're after. We do things just to fill our resumes and increase our network. We want to say, "I went to X university." Or, "I work at X."

No matter what your social status is, you're not better than any other human being. We don't live in the 18th century anymore. No one cares about your social status. People care about your character and skills.

> *"People who hold important positions in society are commonly labelled "somebodies," and their inverse "nobodies"—both of which are, of course, nonsensical descriptors, for we are all, by necessity, individuals with distinct identities and comparable claims on existence."*
>
> *— Alain de Botton*

You Are Not Your Bank Account

Money is awesome. Let's be honest, without it, you can't do much. If you want to get away and live in the woods and be self-sufficient like Thoreau, feel free to do so—no one is stopping you.

But if you want to be a part of society, you need money to survive. However, we give money more power than we should. We let money rule our life's decisions, and that is too much.

The truth is that money comes and goes. I've lost a lot of money in my life, so what? Money is a commodity—don't let it rule you.

"I have no money, no resources, no hopes. I am the happiest man alive."

– Henry Miller

Stop Chasing with Your Eyes Closed

If you're always chasing things that you believe will make you happy, your life will be over in the blink of an eye.

Life is, in contrast to what many of us believe, long enough. As Seneca put it: "Life, if well lived, is long enough."

But we need to learn how to slow down time, and be in the moment, if we want to live well.

Have you ever had a day that you felt like time didn't exist? When you're fully immersed in the moment, time moves slowly. It doesn't matter what you do, if you do it with 100% of your attention, you are not wasting your life.

On the other hand, have you ever thought: "I can't believe a year has passed." We often think that around December 31st of each year, or when it's our birthday.

Call it presence, focus, mindfulness, or whatever you wish. The point is this: You have the power to slow down time—so use it.

All you have to do is live in the moment — free of worry, pressure, and daydreams. When you do that, life is long and time will no longer pass in the blink of an eye.

You're only wasting your life if you're too distracted to experience it.

I believe that, deep down, we all know that we don't have infinite time on our hands. We know that life is not just about earning money, posting your holidays pictures on social media, or the job you have.

It's things like connection, experience, love, relationships, sharing, caring, that we value the most. We all know it, right? But it's not about what you know, it's about what you do.

> *"What you do speaks so loud that I cannot hear what you say."*
> *— Ralph Waldo Emerson*

Work on your character, realize that life is a gift, and enjoy every moment of it—good and bad.

25 THINGS ABOUT LIFE I WISH I HAD KNOWN 10 YEARS AGO

Socrates, considered as one of the founders of Western philosophy, was once named the wisest man on earth by the Oracle of Delphi. When Socrates heard that the oracle had made such a comment, he believed that the statement was wrong.

Socrates said: "I know one thing: that I know nothing."

How can the smartest man on earth know nothing? I heard this paradoxical wisdom for the first time from my school teacher when I was 14 or 15. It made such an impact on me that I used Socrates's quote as my learning strategy.

"I know nothing" to me, means that you might be a wise person, but still, you know nothing. You can learn from everything and everyone.

One thing that I like better than learning from my mistakes is to learn from other people's mistakes. Over the years, I've been blessed to have great mentors, teachers, family, and friends that taught me about life.

What you will find below is a list of the most important things I learned from other people and books. Some of the lessons took me a long time to learn—but if I had to learn these things all by myself, it would take me a lot longer.

We might learn things quickly, but we often forget things at the same rate—and sometimes we need to remind ourselves of the things we've learned.

25 Things About Life I Wish I Had Known 10 Years Ago

Here are 25 of those reminders that others taught me.

1. **Struggle Is Good**. Never say "I can't take it anymore." Say "Bring it on!"
2. **Don't Complain.** Complaining is the biggest waste of time there is. Either do something about it, and if you can't, shut up about it.
3. **Spend Time with People You Love**. That's your family and best friends. If you don't have a family, create one. Most people in life are only visitors. Family is for life.
4. **Don't Start A Relationship If You're Not in Love**. I've done this more than once. You kind of like someone and think: "We might as well give it a shot." Not a good idea. You're either in love, or you are not. Don't fool yourself. It's not fair to you and the other person.
5. **Exercise Daily**. I didn't get this until recently. A healthy body is where you have to start everything in life. If you can't build a healthy and strong body, what CAN you build in life?
6. **Keep a Journal**. No, keeping a journal is not for children. It helps you to become a better thinker and writer. "I don't want to be a writer" you might think. Well, how many emails and texts do you send a day? Everybody is a writer.
7. **Be Grateful**. Say 'thank you' to everyone and everything. "Thank you for this beautiful day." "Thank you for your email." "Thank you for being there for me."
8. **Don't Care About What People Think**. We all die in the end, do you really think it matters what people think of you?
9. **Take More Risks**. Don't be such a wimp.
10. **Pick an Industry, Not A Job**. If you want to become good at something, you need to spend years and years doing that. You can't do that if you hop from industry to industry. Pick an industry you love and start at the bottom. You will find the perfect role for you eventually.

11. **Lead the Way**. When you find yourself in a situation where everyone looks at each other, it's time for you to lead. You're a leader when you decide to become one. There's no initiation or a title. Just a decision.
12. **Money Isn't Important.** It really isn't. But you have to train yourself not to care about money. Don't become too dependent on the stuff you own—otherwise, the stuff will own you.
13. **Be Nice**. I don't mean you should be a pushover. You can be someone that doesn't take shit and be nice about it. Just don't insult people, think you're better than them, or act like an idiot.
14. **Learn Every Day**. You've got to train your brain to stay alert. You don't have to read a book a day to learn every day. Learn from your mistakes. Learn from the people around you—be open to what they can teach you.
15. **Rest Before You Are Tired.** Even if you love your job, and every day seems like a holiday, you need to take time to rest. You're a human and not an android, never forget that.
16. **Don't Judge**. Just because people make different choices than you, they are not stupid. Also, you don't know everything about people, so don't judge them—help them.
17. **Think About Others**. Just be mindful, that's all. We all have families, bills to pay, and our own issues. Don't always make everything about yourself.
18. **Give Without Expecting Something in Return**. Don't keep score. You will become a bitter person if you do that. Give solely for the joy of giving. If you get something in return, great, if you don't, great.
19. **There's No End Game**. We, as species, just *are*. Don't try to figure it all out. Enjoy your journey.
20. **Enjoy Small Things**. I like clichés because they are true. Especially this one. You know why? Everyone says they know it, but no one lives up to it. They just chase big things.

21. **Don't Take Yourself So Seriously**. Yeah, yeah, you're an individual, and people have to take you seriously, I get it. But at the end of the day, we're all a bunch of ants trying to chase the same things. Lighten up.
22. **Don't Blame People**. What's the point? Do you want to punish them? You don't do that to people. Also don't blame yourself—you're only human.
23. **Create Something.** Not to leave a legacy, you won't be here to see it anyway, but to be of use. Make music, write a book, build a table, anything. You'll feel good about yourself, plus you give something back to people to use or enjoy.
24. **Never Look Back Too Long**. Reflecting on the past is only good for one thing: Learning.
25. **Take Action**. Don't just sit there, do something. Without action, there is no outcome.

You might know a lot. But like Socrates, you and I know nothing at all. So we have to keep learning.

SLOW DOWN: YOU'RE NOT FALLING BEHIND

Nothing annoys me more than the loss of time.

When I feel like I'm wasting my time on useless activities, doing meaningless things, or when I'm spending time with negative people, I get frustrated.

When it comes to time, I agree with what Darwin once said:

"A man who dares to waste one hour of time has not discovered the value of life."

But I've found that an obsession with time can put unnecessary pressure on yourself. I see it a lot with ambitious people—anyone who wants to get the most out of life.

They feel like they have to use every single minute of life. Things have to happen: Quick, quick, now, now.

You have to keep pounding forward like a freight train that stops for nothing.

It's great that you want to achieve a lot, and live a life of contribution, but does that mean it has to happen NOW?

But there's a fine line between understanding the value of time, and being impatient.

One of my mentors is an entrepreneur in his late forties. When I recently told him I get impatient, he told me he's exactly the same. He said:

"Impatience makes smart people do stupid things."

We all try to get ahead. We work hard. Put all our energy and love in relationships. We work on ourselves—our character.

But sometimes, we feel like we've fallen behind.

- "I'm still sharing an apartment with 3 strangers."
- "I'm not married yet."
- "We still don't have kids."
- "My business still hasn't taken off."
- "I didn't get my big break yet."
- "I'm still waiting to become a manager."
- "I'm stuck in the same job for years."
- "I'm not losing weight."

I don't want to pretend I'm past that. We all have those feelings. And the higher you move up the ladder, the higher your standards become.

When I was in college, I couldn't wait to get out so I could get my own place and stop sharing a dirty old apartment with three other guys. And when I started earning money, I got a place of my own.

But a few years later, when I moved to London from Holland, I had to give up my two-bedroom apartment with a roof terrace to live in an apartment that was smaller, *and* that I had to share with a stranger. It felt like I was back at square one.

Take a step back. There's nothing wrong with that.

Switching careers, education, cities, are all hard. In a way, you *are* taking a step back momentarily. But you'll bounce back. That's hard to remind yourself when you're in the moment.

When I was in college, I had a marketing professor who used to be a physician. Yes, that means he studied nine or ten years to become a general practitioner. Then, he worked as a GP for a decade.

And in his forties, he decided he didn't want to be a doctor anymore. He was always passionate about business and marketing. So he pursued a Master's degree in business administration, and later he got a PhD in marketing. I think that whole process took him six or seven years.

And when he was my professor, he was in his late fifties. But the guy looked twenty years younger, and was full of energy. He truly loved what he did. Plus, he was proud of the long road he took.

The road that you travelled turns you into the person you are today.

I meet a lot of people in their twenties who are frustrated that life is not exactly the way they want. I even meet people in their thirties and forties like that.

It's a universal thing. And that thing is called impatience.

Like my mentor said, you do stupid things when you're impatient.

- Do you really need to buy a house?
- Do you really want to get married?
- Do you really want to take that promotion?
- Do you really have to sell your business?
- Do you really love your job?
- Do you really have to take on that client?

Don't do all these things because you always wanted to do those things. Don't do things because you're afraid of the alternative.

Because the alternative is ALWAYS harder.

- "Shit! Does that mean I have to work for free?"
- "Does that mean I have to start all over?"
- "What?! I can't be single."
- "Does that mean I have to study for years?"

YES.

But hardship defines you and your character.

So suit up, forget about the fast train, step in a car, and prepare yourself for one LONG ride that's called life.

But remember: Drive slow.

HOW TO FIND MENTORS

Before there were books, universities, or classes, there were mentorships to pass on wisdom and knowledge. In the west, mentorships existed since the Ancient Greek times—it's a tried method of learning.

Sometimes people mix up apprenticeships and mentorships. An apprenticeship is basically an internship, which is a system that was created in the Middle Ages.

If you wanted to become a tailor, baker, or merchant, you became an apprentice first and learned the craft on the job.

The main difference between the two is that mentorships are informal. And that's exactly what makes it difficult to find a mentor.

Most people understand the value of mentors, but finding one is not easy. I also didn't have mentors until I was out of college.

But in the past six years, I've been lucky to cross paths with three great people, who became mentors to me, and taught me invaluable lessons.

There are also several other people that I speak to every once in a while—we exchange ideas, and share knowledge—they are also like mentors. So mentors come in many types of relationships.

Here are seven things I learned about finding a mentor.

1. Become A Learning Machine

Before you start thinking about finding a mentor, you want to think about two things:

- What's your field?
- What can you bring to the table?

It's astonishing to me that people want to find a mentor without any sense of direction. For example: If you want to work in sports, it doesn't make sense to find a mentor who's in art (unless you want to bring art to sports).

If you're looking for someone who grabs you by the hand and tells you about life, you don't need a mentor—you need experience.

And you only get experience by doing things. You can't expect that people hand you everything—that's not what a mentor does.

First, decide what industry you want to work in. Second, study that industry. Before you find real-life mentors, your mentors are books, degrees, courses, YouTube videos, or any other source of knowledge.

You need basic knowledge of life *and* your field if you want to find a mentor. No one's waiting for a puppy that they have to raise.

It's important to bring something to the table before you approach potential mentors.

2. Work on Your Emotional Intelligence

Because of the informal nature of mentorships, you need emotional intelligence if you want to find a mentor.

Emotional intelligence can be defined in many ways, and my definition is this: Don't be annoying.

If you have a mentor, you will spend time with her—and because it's informal, it all comes down to likeability.

Likeability is also something that some companies stress upon during interviews. Because they know they will spend a lot of time with people who join their company, they ask themselves a version of this question: "Would I hang out with this person?"

If you don't want to be annoying, here are some tips:

- Don't try to be someone you are not
- Don't think you know it all
- Be honest and humble
- Don't try too hard
- Tell stories

Basically, do whatever Dale Carnegie writes in *How To Win Friends And Influence People*.

3. Don't Ask

Let's get down to the practical stuff. If there's someone you look up to, and you want to learn from, it's time to approach her. You can find people who could mentor you everywhere.

Don't just think of influential people — look in your family, the family of your friends, friends of your friends, etc. Look close. That will make it easier to connect.

But you don't call or email someone and say: "Will you be my mentor?" People will probably think you're delusional. Most people don't mind helping others, but it also can't be a one-way street.

If you're contacting someone for the first time, try to keep it short and simple. You can ask a simple question, or give them praise. You don't want to ask for anything big.

Also, please don't email people and offer them coffee in exchange for free advice. Anyone can buy coffee, but not everyone actually can bring something valuable to the table. You have to be compelling for someone to spend time with you.

4. Add Value

When the other person responds to you, start thinking about adding value to them. You can do that by researching them or their company.

And if you want to add value, you need #1 on this list. You can't add much value if you don't have knowledge or experience.

Offer them help, create something, give them ideas, anything—be proactive.

5. Be Mindful of The Other Person's Time

Always keep in mind that the other person doesn't owe you anything and never will. You're looking for a mutual relationship.

If you ever want to set up a meeting, do it whenever *they* have time and wherever *they* are.

It shows that you're serious about learning, will do whatever it takes, and most importantly; that you have emotional intelligence.

6. Take Your Craft Seriously

If you're approaching someone who's successful in what they do, it's very likely that they take their job seriously.

You want to meet them with the same intensity and passion (also, don't fake it or try to find a mentor so you can tell others about it).

One of my mentors told me early on: "I meet a lot of annoying, negative, people who just work to get a paycheck. What's the fun of being around those people?"

It might seem like a fair assumption that everybody takes their job seriously, but that's not always the case. However, if you *do* take your craft seriously, that can be very infectious.

7. Stay in Touch

Because you don't ask people to become your mentor, you want to put it differently. If you can tell that they enjoyed meeting with you, you can say:

"This was very useful. If you feel the same, do you want to make this a recurring thing?"

Be prepared to hear a no. Some people might be busy or focused on a project. Take it graciously and say you understand, but don't go into hiding. Try to send them relevant things in the future.

Finally, when it comes to frequency: I speak to my mentors every 2–3 months. And in between meetings we sometimes exchange emails—for things like book recommendations, articles, or questions.

Unless you have the opportunity to work together on a frequent basis, you don't need to meet your mentor every week because you want to take their advice and apply it.

So give it some time. But try to keep the momentum by staying in touch via email or text messages.

These are my tips. I don't know all the answers, and this is not a clear-cut blueprint—don't expect to find one anywhere either.

Finding a mentor is a not a formal thing, so don't treat it like one. Mentorship is like friendship, and that's what your mentor eventually becomes: Your friend. Always keep that in mind.

HOW TO BUILD THE SELF-CONFIDENCE YOU NEED TO WIN AT LIFE

Do you ever feel shitty about yourself? It happens all the time to most of us.

It seems like everyone is building billion-dollar businesses, becoming YouTube stars, or making it big on Instagram.

Deep down, most of us also know that it's 99% bullshit. But at the same time, we see all these people living awesome lives, and we don't care if it's real or not.

Whether you want money, fame, travel, or none of that stuff, it doesn't matter because it always comes down to this: How confident are you?

- Are you confident enough to say "fuck it," and pursue you dream?
- Are you confident enough to say "fuck all this bullshit, I don't need it," and stay grounded?

You see? Self-confidence is important if you want to win at life—no matter what you're after, a lack of confidence will always hold you back.

Research even shows that lack of self-confidence is associated with:

- Depression
- Loneliness and feeling left out
- Lower academic achievement
- Lower life satisfaction

I've researched self-confidence for years, and the most practical theory that I've found is something called 'confidence by competence.'

In 1952, Bernice Milburn Moore published an article called 'Self-Confidence for Competence' in the *Journal of Educational Leadership*. In the article, she discusses self-confidence for teachers, but I've found it useful in all settings of life.

If you look up the definition of self-confidence, you always get more or less the same description. Moore describes it as "a trust in self, a faith in one's ability to be able to meet situations as they may arise."

But more importantly, she says:

> *"Self-confidence without competence is of as little use as is competence without self-confidence."*

It means this: Going to business school is competence. But using your business competence to lead a company is self-confidence plus competence. They are only useful when combined.

That analogy goes both ways. Just confidence in yourself, without the competence, is also useless—talking the talk is not a sustainable strategy.

You need the talk and bravado, but you also need to develop the skills to back up your talk.

Building Your Self-Confidence

So you become more self-confident if you become better at what you do. That's the system, and it's backed by research.

How can you use this information? The following process is

easy—but completing the steps takes hard work.

It goes like this:

1. Improve your competencies
2. Put them into practice
3. See results
4. Grow more confident
5. Repeat

That's the process.

"That's great and all, but what if I don't see results? Plus, I don't have the time to practice."

If you want to make excuses, that's fine. It's your life. But this method of building self-confidence is based on real, tangible steps, and not intangible stuff like affirmations. Confidence doesn't appear magically by itself.

You can tell yourself every day that you're confident, lucky to be alive, or whatever—but if you lack the skills to get shit done, you'll never truly believe in yourself.

And that's my biggest issue with a lot of self-help theory and writers. Yes, affirmations, positive thinking, goal setting, is all great, but it's NOTHING without execution.

How can you expect to build confidence if you never do anything? It's impossible.

> *"Nothing builds self-esteem and self-confidence like accomplishment."*
>
> —*Thomas Carlyle*

"What competencies should I improve?"

That depends on what you're after. But there are also some skills that I believe every person can benefit from.

- **Emotional intelligence**—Research shows that humans are inherently social. Without good relationships, we die. And if you want good relationships, you need emotional intelligence: Understanding other people's emotions and how to respond to them. This is something you can learn.

- **Self-awareness**—You can practice self-awareness by continuous self-reflection. Write down your thoughts; try to understand why you do what you do, what you can do better, and what you're doing well. Know yourself.

- **Problem-solving**—Our current school system dates from the industrial revolution. We're trained to become cogs in a wheel. We're not trained to solve problems in complex situations—instead, we do what we are told. But the world has changed and in the current state, the person that is better at problem-solving will win.

Don't fool yourself into thinking that your life will be better as long as you wish for it.

When you put in work and see the results—like a stronger body, more energy, more money, or whatever you're after—you start believing in your ability to get shit done.

Now go out there, do things, get better at them, see results, repeat that process and grow more confident.

5 WAYS TO BUILD A THICKER SKIN SO YOU CAN GO THROUGH LIFE SMILING

Do you ever feel hurt by what people say about you? Well, it's a part of life, so you better get used to it.

I'm amazed by how quickly people get upset. And I'm not talking about getting upset about real things like disease, death, or not having food.

I'm talking about the small stuff of daily life. Why are our feelings hurt when the littlest things happen?

- Someone disagrees with you.
- A coworker says something bad about you.
- Someone always is 'lucky' and you are not.
- Your friend stabs you in the back.
- You don't like your job.
- People don't like your art.

So what?

In the past, I would get hurt by those things.

"Anne said that about me? What the fuck? My life is over." That's what I said when I found out that my first ex-girlfriend said bad stuff about me years ago. As a youngster, you think your life is over fairly quickly, especially with those kinds of shenanigans.

But then I got over it. Come on—you can't get upset about nonsense.

I see it all the time.

- Bloggers get their feelings hurt and start writing about how they have to deal with criticism.
- I see friends who don't start working on their dream because someone close to them said they couldn't do it.
- People I work with never take the plunge because they are afraid of the potential criticism.

Why would you listen, or even care? Earnest Hemingway, considered as one of the best authors of all time (and one of my favorite writers), said this in his memoir *A Moveable Feast*:

"He started talking about my writing and I stopped listening."

If you want to live your life like that, you need a thick skin to tune out the voices outside of you.

Because what happens when you get upset or let other people get the best of you? You might give up what you do—you question yourself. Or maybe you start changing yourself for the worse—you stop being yourself.

Having a thick skin is important—especially if you want to go through life smiling. Here's how I've grown a thick skin over the years.

1. Don't Shy Away from Confrontation

I'm all about kindness. But I'm also about not taking any shit.

A few years ago, I found out that one of my coworkers wasn't honest to upper management. I kept quiet. I was afraid of the confrontation. And that was a huge mistake because that idiot caused a lot of damage to the people in that company.

I don't want to be Superman, who always comes to the rescue. But if something unjust happens, I'm doing something about it. Maybe it backfires, but at least I did the right thing.

Also, if people treat me unfairly, I tell it to them straight. I don't get angry. It's not cool to treat people badly. I just let my moral compass speak for me.

You don't have to be kind 100% of the time.

If people screw me, or others over, I'm not going to just let it slide.

The more you stand up for yourself and others, the better you get at it. You will find out that it's not a big deal. Confrontation doesn't mean you have to fight people with your fists, do it with your words or actions. And always keep calm.

2. It's Never Personal

Aw poor you, someone stabbed you in the back at work. But you know what? It's not personal. Honestly.

I don't want to justify bad behavior. But never forget that the other person is doing it to get ahead. That's what people do.

Even though life is not a zero-sum game, life still remains a competition. We compete for attention, love, money, jobs.

If you lose, or someone doesn't like you, it's not personal. They don't know you. Why would you question yourself?

- Am I really a bad friend?
- Am I a bad person?
- No one likes me.

That's your mind coming up with weird stuff. I prefer to look at things for what they are. Life is a competition and sometimes you lose—that's all.

Get over it. Don't start losing faith in mankind all of a sudden. Nothing is personal. The world doesn't revolve around you.

> *"Let us try to teach generosity and altruism, because we are born selfish."*
>
> *—Richard Dawkins*

3. Express Yourself Online

People online give you their unfiltered opinion. Yes, you can hide behind your computer and maybe it's stupid sometimes. But that's also a good thing.

In real life, people are never 100% honest with you. Especially not your friends and family.

If you want to get some real feedback, go and publish something online. Write a piece on Medium. Start a discussion on Reddit. Upload a video on YouTube. And read the comments.

If you don't get any comments, ask for them. Approach people one-on-one and ask for their opinion. Or put up a link on a forum and ask people for their opinion.

If people like you, great, if they don't, so what?

4. Put Things in Perspective

According to the most recent statistics, 12.7 percent of the world's population lived at or below $1.90 a day.

What was that again? Someone yelled at you? Or someone said something nasty to you on the internet?

Every time I get slightly upset about things, I remind myself how lucky I am. I'm healthy, and I have food and shelter. That's all you need.

5. You Don't HAVE to Be Liked By Everyone

I recently met a person who said that Gandhi was just an attention seeker. Can you believe that? And so was Nelson Mandela, MLK, or any other historical figure, according to him.

The guy who said that is a real idiot. And I never bother responding to idiots (online and offline).

If people don't like Gandhi, don't expect that everyone does like *you*. It's impossible. So why strive for impossible things?

It's not a "you can't build an airplane" type of impossible. Like I've said before, never let rules hold you back.

But some things will NEVER happen. One of those things is *being liked by every person in the world.*

So don't sweat it. And that's what you do when you have a thick skin: Never sweat and always smile.

HOW TO READ 100 BOOKS A YEAR

Does your reading list keep growing? Did you buy books that you've never read? It might be time to cross more books from your list this year than ever.

If you're reading less than you want, you're not the only one. One year ago I looked at my Goodreads page and noticed that I had read only five books in 2014. That realization frustrated me.

I love books, but since I graduated from college in 2011, I'd been reading fewer books every single year. My work and life got in the way of reading as much as I wanted.

Why read 100 books in a year? You read because you want to learn from other people's experience. Otto von Bismarck put it best:

> *"Fools learn from experience. I prefer to learn from the experience of others."*

If you want to get anywhere in this world, you need to educate yourself, and to educate yourself you need to read—a lot.

Here's how to do it.

1. Buy in Bulk

It costs money to buy books, and it costs you time to read them—I'm assuming you have both if you're reading this.

Everyone can make time. And if you don't have money, find a way to make or save money.

As Dutch Renaissance man Erasmus once said:

> *"When I have a little money, I buy books; and if I have any left, I buy food and clothes."*

Be assured, the money and time you spend on books are worth it. I can't think of a better investment. Books are only a waste of money if you don't read them.

If you want to read more, you have to buy more books. Some people don't get it. They spend $200 on new shoes, but they find it ridiculous to buy 20 books from Amazon.

The idea is simple: If you have more books in your house, you'll have more choices, and this will help you read more.

Here's why: Most of the books you read are not planned in advance. You don't sit down in January and say: "The first week of June I'll read this book."

You finish a book, look you at your inventory, and decide what to read next. Don't overthink which book you should read next—you'll end up reading reviews for hours, which is a waste of time.

For example, most people who want to start with Stoicism ask me: "Which one should I read first—Seneca, Marcus Aurelius or Epictetus?"

Buy them all. Read them all.

Having an inventory of books keeps up the momentum. You also never have an excuse *not* to read.

2. A(lways) B(e) R(eading)

You might have heard of the term *'ABC'* from the play/movie *Glengarry Glen Ross*: Always Be Closing. Many salespeople and entrepreneurs live by that motto.

I live by a different motto: *Always Be Reading*.

I read a minimum of 1 hour per day on weekdays and even more during the weekend and holidays.

Find a way to read around your schedule and your life situation. Don't make excuses like you're tired or too busy.

Always Be Reading means that you:

- Read on the train
- Read while you're breastfeeding your baby
- Read while you're eating
- Read at the doctor's office
- Read at work
- And most importantly — read while everyone else is wasting their time watching the news or checking Facebook for the 113th time that day.

If you do that, you'll read more than 100 books in a year. Here's how. Most people read 50 pages an hour. If you read 10 hours a week, you'll read 26,000 pages a year. Let's say the average book you read is 250 pages: In this scenario, you'll read 104 books in a year.

With that pace—even if you take a two-week break—you'll read at least 100 books in a year.

That's a good return on your time investment. What's the ROI of reading the news? I don't know exactly, but it must be negative.

3. Read Relevant Books Only

Have you ever read a book that's supposedly amazing and you don't get it? I wouldn't go as far as saying that any book sucks, because people spend a lot of time writing and editing a book.

But not all books are for everyone. A book might be a bestseller, but maybe you can't stand the writing. Or maybe it's not the right time to read a book.

In any case: If you can't flip through the pages, put the book away and pick up something you are so excited about that you tear up the pages.

Read books that are close to what's going on in your life. There's a book for everything you can think off. People are writing books for 2000 years, and there have been plenty of people in your shoes: struggling teen, aspiring artist, broke entrepreneur, new parent, etc.

Don't waste your time reading about subjects you have zero interest in.

Instead, pick out the books that are related to your profession or hobby. Read books about people that you admire. Don't read a book just because it's a best-seller or a classic if it has no meaning to you.

4. Read Multiple Books Simultaneously

There are no rules to reading so you can do whatever you want. At times, I'm reading 5 books at once. I might read 50 pages of one book in the morning and then read another book in the afternoon.

That's how I prefer it. Others like to read a book cover to cover and only then read something new.

If you're reading something that's complicated, you might want to read something that's easier for the evenings. I like to read biographies before I go to sleep because they are like stories. Fiction also works well in the evening.

I don't want to read a book about investing in bed with a highlighter and a pen. If I do that, I will be awake until 3 AM because my mind is buzzing with the new things I'm learning.

5. Retain the Knowledge

Knowledge is only good if you use it. To retain knowledge, you need a system that helps you do that. This is how I do it:

- When you read a book, use a pen to make notes in the margins and highlight important text. If you're reading digitally, be aware of over-highlighting. Just because it's so easy you shouldn't highlight everything you find slightly interesting. Keep the highlighting for 'aha' things only.
- If you read something you want to definitely remember, fold the top or bottom corner of the page. For digital readers: take a picture and store it in a notetaking app you prefer.
- When you finish the book, go back to the pages with the folds and skim your notes.
- Write down (use your notetaking software or physical notebook) in your own words what the book is about and what advice the author is giving.
- Copy the quotes that stand out the most to you.

The point is not to copy the book but to help you process the information so you can use it later.

Read as much as you possibly can—but never forget to apply what you've learned because that is what counts the most. You put in many hours to read books, make sure you get something out of it.

ACKNOWLEDGEMENTS

When I was 16, I read *'The 48 Laws of Power'* by Robert Greene. Even though I could not relate to most of the book, I did get the overall message. With his book, Greene wanted to show us that we can learn how to get into a position of power. I thought to myself, "if you can learn power, you can learn anything." In the next years, I studied books on seduction, fear, psychology, success, influence, and many more success-related topics. However, I never thought of writing a book myself.

It was not until early 2015 when I considered writing a book. I lived in London at the time, and I had just lost my grandmother, who was very dear to me. I also broke up with my girlfriend at the same time. Furthermore, I started disliking my job at an American corporation because of office politics.

But when you look at my situation from the outside, it looked fine. I had a job that offered good pay, pension and enough opportunities to promote internally. However, I felt unmotivated and unhappy. Fortunately, not for long. I discovered that the only way out of a negative mindset was to conquer my fear forever. I had overcome my fears in the past as well, but I was not consistent—fear manifested in self-doubt sometimes.

Despite that, I have always been quite fearless. I travelled the world, worked in or with companies in Shanghai, New York, Miami, London, Barcelona, and Los Angeles. I took bold moves in my career and relationships.

However, I did have deeply rooted fears. I was afraid of being alone, being rejected, and I did not believe in my ability to solve any problem that life would throw at me. Nevertheless, with all the actionable advice I talked about in this book, I managed to defeat fear and do what I am passionate about: help other people to live the life they want.

This book would not be possible without my brother, Daniel Foroux. He served as the primary editor of this book. His input for this book proved to be of immense value. I also want to thank my parents for their support and insightful discussions. I have to thank my friends Derek and Koert; they played an important role in the editing process of this book.

I have been blessed to meet a lot of inspiring people over the world. I have learned a lot from our interactions and deep conversations about life. I want to thank everyone that I had an openhearted discussion with about what motivates them. Without deep connections with other people this book could not have been written.

READING LIST

If you like to read more about topics I discussed in this book, I can recommend to read the following books. The books that I have listed below are books I think every person who wants to improve their life should read. I hope you enjoy them.

Entrepreneurship & Business

The 4-Hour Work Week by Tim Ferriss
The modern entrepreneur's bible. This book changed my perspective on doing business. Tim Ferriss has influenced thousands of people over the world who have gone to start companies themselves. Ferriss is also an angel investor and an advisor to Facebook, Twitter, Evernote, and Uber, and other tech companies. This is a must read for anyone who desires financial freedom.

Zero to One by Peter Thiel and Blake Masters
Peter Thiel is mostly known as the co-founder of PayPal and the first outside investor to Facebook. *Zero to One* is a book that discusses the motives behind entrepreneurship. It covers essential topics such as history, human behavior, competition, creativity, and how new tech companies change the world. *Zero to One* is a necessary read for every entrepreneur or anyone who is interested in learning about the rise of startups.

The Magic of Thinking Big by Dr. David Schwartz

Thinking big is essential for every entrepreneur, salesperson or marketer. We let small thinking obstruct hitting high goals in life. *The Magic of Thinking Big* gives you useful methods that you can use in everyday life. Dr. Schwartz presents techniques that you can also use in your personal life. This book can also be placed in the 'Personal Growth' category. It is an excellent all-around book on positive thinking. The practical advice makes it easy to apply the techniques in your personal and professional life.

Marketing

Purple Cow by Seth Godin

This is one of the best books on marketing and Seth Godin is considered as one of the best marketing minds in the world. The book's message is simple: if you want to stand out from the crowd, you have to be remarkable. *Purple Cow* is a must-read for every business owner and marketer. I also encourage you to read Godin's personal blog. He posts a thought-provoking article every single day. Now, that is remarkable.

Contagious by Jonah Berger

When you want to have massive marketing success with a limited budget, read *Contagious* by Jonah Berger. It is an excellent book with a thorough analysis of viral campaigns, and why they catch on. Jonah Berger is a Marketing professor at the Wharton School at the University of Pennsylvania and uses scientific research to back up his findings. His writing style, however, is far from academic and very enjoyable.

Stoicism

Meditations by Marcus Aurelius

Marcus Aurelius (emperor of Rome 161 - 180 AD) is one of the three famous modern Stoics, the two others are Seneca and Epictetus. As the ruler of the largest empire of the world, Aurelius had great responsibility and power. He wrote *Meditations* for his personal use. It consists of lessons he learned and notes he made to himself about living and dealing with people. This book changed the way I look at life. Reading this book made me a better thinker. It also made me realize that we have less control than we think. In fact, we do not control anything but our own actions and response. A must read for every human being.

On the Shortness of Life by Seneca

Seneca rose to prominence in Rome while pursuing a career in the courts and politics. He spent eight years in exile, allegedly for an affair with an emperor's sister. When he was recalled in AD 49, he was appointed tutor to the boy who would become the emperor Nero in AD 54. In his time as emperor, Nero appointed Seneca as an unofficial chief minister. In AD 65, Seneca was compelled by Nero to commit suicide because of an alleged plot against Nero. *In the Shortness of Life*, Seneca writes about the art of living. This short book is highly recommended for everyone. Seneca teaches us that life is short and that we have to live our life to the fullest.

The Obstacle Is the Way by Ryan Holiday

Inspired by Marcus Aurelius' *Mediations*, Ryan Holiday wrote an excellent book about how we can turn our adversity into advantage. The book is full of stories about how icons of history dealt with their obstacles. Ryan argues that we should not shy away from obstacles, but rather deal with obstacles as a way of life. Hence, the title of the book, "The Obstacle

Is the Way". This book is well written and is a modern take on stoicism.

Personal Growth

How To Win Friends And Influence People by Dale Carnegie

An all-time classic when it comes to personal development. This book is an essential read for everyone—particularly for people getting out of college. Carnegie writes about how you can increase your popularity, persuade people, make friends, enable you to win new clients and customers, become a better speaker and boost enthusiasm among your colleagues. He gives advice that is crucial for your success in the professional world. This book teaches you techniques that you can use in social interactions with other people. Whatever we want to do in life, we need to work with other persons. Carnegie shows you how to deal with people in an effective way.

The Greatest Salesman in The World by Og Mandino

While the title sounds like a sales book, *The Greatest Salesman in The World* is more a philosophy book. The first part of the book is a parable set in the time just prior to Christianity. The second part consists of ten scrolls that teach you to believe in yourself and the work you are doing. It is a book that also shows you how to create a habit. Og Mandino writes that you have to reread every scroll, three times a day, for a month. That will take you ten months to complete this book. This book is an excellent example of the power of priming and positivity. Academy Award winner Matthew McConaughey said this book changed his life and got him into acting.

Finances

Rich Dad, Poor Dad by Robert Kiyosaki

Unfortunately, we do not learn how to deal with money at school. *Rich Dad, Poor Dad* is a required reading for anyone who starts making money. The younger the better. Moreover, for adults, if you think that your house is an asset, Robert Kiyosaki tells you to rethink that. He claims that a house is a liability. Making money is one thing, keeping it and growing it something else. This book teaches us financial literacy.

The Essays of Warren Buffett by Warren Buffett

Warren Buffett is one of the greatest investors in history. This book offers a collection of his "chairman's letter" (his personal progress report) to Berkshire Hathaway shareholders at their annual meeting. Learn from the best investor how to invest in stocks. This book offers a unique insight into the mind of an investor. Recommended reading for anyone who wants to invest in the stock market.

Creativity

The War of Art by Steven Pressfield

Being creative requires discipline. Steven Pressfield argues that 'resistance' stands in the way of people who want to create something in life. The book discusses this enemy that every one of us must face. Pressfield presents a battle plan to conquer this internal foe and shows how to achieve success. *The War of Art* is excellent reading for writers, entrepreneurs, actors, dancers, painters, photographers, filmmakers, and other creative people.

The Icarus Deception by Seth Godin

The world has changed, and conformity no longer leads to security. Seth Godin argues in The Icarus Deception that creativity is scarce and more valuable than ever. Godin encourages everyone to make art. By adopting an artistic attitude, we can add value to other people's life. We have to be problem solvers, and conformity does not solve problems. Creative thinking does. An exceptional book to adopt the creative mindset.

Biography

Man's Search for Meaning by Victor Frankl

Viktor Frankl was a psychiatrist before the war. His ability to observe the behavior of his fellow prisoners in Auschwitz resulted *in Man's Search for Meaning*. This unique book describes how we choose our attitude in any given set of circumstances. Even during the horrible conditions of a concentration camp, humans can endure the suffering and find meaning in living because of inner decisions. This outstanding work offers us a peek into human suffering and in the art of living. The book consists of two parts. The first part is a memoir while the second part describes Frankl's Logotherapy. This is a treatment he used on his patients and described ways to find meaning in life.

Total Recall by Arnold Schwarzenegger

Arnold Schwarzenegger's story is remarkable. A boy from a small town in Austria turned into a bodybuilding champion. A bodybuilder turned into one of the biggest Hollywood stars in history. An actor turned into Governor. This unique story is worth reading. Schwarzenegger also shares his life lessons in *Total Recall*. A great read for anyone who wants to get a glimpse into how the mind of a successful person works.

Fitness & Health

Bigger, Leaner, Stronger by Michael Matthews

The only book you need for improving your fitness. Matthews has written a complete book that focusses on simplicity. We all hate complicated fitness and eating regiments. *Bigger, Leaner, Stronger* is based on a few simple methods and destroys many popular fitness myths.

Spark by John Ratey

Everyone knows that exercise is good for our health. However, it can also transform your mind. This book is based on scientific research and teaches us how to boost brain cells, protect ourselves against mental illness and dementia, and ensure success in exams and the workplace. A great read that inspires us to live an active lifestyle.

NEWSLETTER

Every week I send an email to subscribers of the dariusforoux.com newsletter, which contains:

- Recommendations for inspirational books, blog posts, movies, and podcasts
- Exclusive peeks of my upcoming books and courses
- A summary of the articles I've published

The members of this newsletter form a community to share knowledge and provide feedback.

If you want to join the list, all you need to do is send me an email: dariusforoux@gmail.com. Mention 'Newsletter' in the subject.

Or you can go to my website, www.dariusforoux.com/newsletter, to signup for the list.

PRL/6 3/4/25

pp. 68-75